100ESSENTIAL**FUNK** GROOVES**FOR**GUITAR

Master the Styles of the Funk Guitar Legends – From Jimmy Nolen to Cory Wong

STEVE**ALLSWORTH**

FUNDAMENTAL**CHANGES**

100 Essential Funk Grooves for Guitar

Master the Styles of the Funk Guitar Legends – From Jimmy Nolen to Cory Wong

ISBN: 978-1-78933-387-9

Published by **www.fundamental-changes.com**

www.fundamental-changes.com

Over 12,000 fans on Facebook: **FundamentalChangesInGuitar**

Instagram: **FundamentalChanges**

For over 350 Free Guitar Lessons with Videos Check Out

www.fundamental-changes.com

Cover Image Copyright: Shutterstock, Robert Kirby

Special thanks:

To Jevon Beaumont for laying down some low-end stank

Contents

Introduction

Like many guitarists, I grew up on a diet of the usual Blues/Rock suspects: B.B. King, Clapton, SRV, Angus Young, Hendrix, Eddie Van Halen and Joe Satriani. However, the one musical style that has taught me the most about groove and playing with other musicians is Funk. That magical moment when the whole band exists inside "the pocket" is truly hard to beat. The musical tentacles of Funk reach into so many different genres that it's difficult to overestimate its influence. Whatever your musical background, Funk can feed into all aspects of your playing, from holding down a basic rhythm to helping to develop groove in your soloing.

In this book, I'll take you through the playing styles of the truly great Funk players, all the way from the James Brown era guitarists Jimmy Nolen and Catfish Collins, to modern players such as Cory Wong and Adam Smirnoff. Each chapter is based around a sub-genre of Funk and includes a gear checklist and recommended listening. There's even an accompanying Spotify playlist to help with your immersion into the world of Funk. The more listening you do, the more this style will permeate your playing. It'll also really help you to hear/see the timeline and musical connection between all the guitarists we'll be looking at.

We'll dig into the sound, rhythms, technique and compositional approach of each player – all with meticulously recorded backing tracks for you to play along to. This isn't a simple set of player pastiches, however, it's a deep dive into each player's approach. Understanding how they developed their ideas will enable you to come up with *your own* improvised ideas and broaden your palette of rhythmic vocabulary, all while developing that mystical *pocket*.

How to use this book

You'll find a combination of TAB, scale/chord boxes and the occasional diagram to help you navigate each of the 100 examples. There will always be a point of focus for each example (e.g., rhythm, picking/fretting hand technique, genre/style, compositional approach and arrangement) and quite often there'll be an underlying theoretical concept. Ultimately, this is to help you come up with your own ideas, whether that's working with the backing tracks, in a live band environment, or putting together your own original songs. As you get more comfortable with the ideas, you can begin to develop, adapt and own them. I'd also thoroughly recommend recording yourself playing along with the backing tracks (or even just a metronome), as this can provide great insight into your playing.

I've tried not to be too heavy-handed with the theory, but there is a certain level of assumed knowledge that you'll need to get you started with the concepts we're dealing with. As a minimum, a basic working knowledge of the following will really help:

- Diatonic major and minor harmony

- Roman Numerals for chord numbering (e.g., I ii iii IV V etc.)

- Common major scale modes (e.g., Ionian, Dorian, Mixolydian, Aeolian)

- Intervals (e.g., major 3rd, perfect 5th etc.)

There are also tone tips and pickup suggestions to help capture the sound of each player, alongside their usual guitar/amp combinations. A lot of the sound comes from the hands/feel of each player, of course, so if you only have one guitar and none of the amps mentioned, don't worry (although a single coil guitar such as a Strat will help!)

Finally, one of the most essential components when coming up with your own ideas is *active listening*. Almost every example in this book is based around the idea of finding space, so developing a good ear for how your guitar parts interact with other instruments is essential practice.

And don't forget… *if it cooks, let it burn.*

Steve.

Get the Spotify playlist to accompany this book now by scanning the QR code

Get the Audio

The audio files for this book are available to download for free from **www.fundamental-changes.com.** The link is in the top right-hand corner. Click on the "Guitar" link then simply select this book title from the drop-down menu and follow the instructions to get the audio.

We recommend that you download the files directly to your computer, not to your tablet, and extract them there before adding them to your media library. You can then put them onto your tablet, iPod or burn them to CD. On the download page there are instructions, and we also provide technical support via the contact form.

For over 350 free guitar lessons with videos check out:

www.fundamental-changes.com

Join our free Facebook Community of Cool Musicians

www.facebook.com/groups/fundamentalguitar

Tag us for a share on Instagram: **FundamentalChanges**

Chapter One – James Brown-era Funk

The main players: Jimmy Nolen, Catfish Collins, Hearlon "Cheese" Martin.

Chapter Overview: Dominant 9 and 13 chords, chicken scratch technique, integrating the Mixolydian and Dorian scales, cross rhythms.

All forms of Funk lead back to the pioneer and *Godfather of Soul,* James Brown. "Mr Dynamite" was largely responsible for two revolutions in 20th century music. Not only was he crucial in helping RnB develop into Soul, but he singlehandedly helped transform Soul into Funk. In the mid-1960s, Brown started to experiment with the syncopated rhythms and danceable grooves of New Orleans Jazz. Less emphasis was placed on melody and harmony in favour of chants/shouts, riffs and static chord progressions. Up until Brown's first foray into this style with *Out of Sight,* RnB, Soul and Motown music had emphasised the *backbeat* (beats two and four) but the classic James Brown signature groove was developed to emphasise the *downbeat,* with a heavy emphasis on the "one". This emphasis of the first beat allowed for syncopation to occur in the "gaps" that followed.

Although James Brown had several great musicians in his band over the years, the rhythmic formula remained largely the same. Simplicity and space were absolutely crucial, and each musical part inhabited its own rhythmic space, while being completely locked in and connected to the rest. In this style of Funk, you'll generally never hear two intertwining guitar parts playing the same rhythmic idea; instead one will play in counterpoint to the other. Most of the guitar parts rarely step away from the same rhythmic figure (and often the same chord) for the whole song.

Sixteen or so guitarists added their unique flavour to the "James Brown sound" between 1956-1976. While each deserves their place in our hall of fame, we can't possibly cover them all here, so I've focused instead on the key figures who helped shape Funk guitar for the next half century.

Jimmy Nolen is undoubtedly one of the most important figures in Funk guitar and was one of Brown's most prolific guitarists over two periods, from 1965-1970 and 1972-1983. Although each of the great guitarists who followed made a significant contribution to Brown's magic formula, Nolen's was the blueprint that they (and literally almost all Funk guitarists to date) followed. He developed the infamous "chicken scratch" technique that was first heard on *Papa's Got a Brand New Bag* – a thin, cutting sound that was as much about lightness of touch in the fretting hand and picking close to bridge as it was choice of amp and guitar. Nolen also pioneered syncopated single-note Funk, something that came to dominate much of the '70s and '80s.

Nolen's signature sound is extremely punchy to cut through the huge sound of the band. A key part of this sound is created by cranking the treble on a Fender Twin. He mainly used a Gibson E-175 and ES-5 Switchmaster, both hollow-body jazz guitars fitted with single coil P-90s, which gave his sound a very slight breakup rather than glassy cleans. In the mid 1970s he was also seen sporting an Acoustic Black Widow (Hendrix and Zappa also used this brand), a guitar with a bit more output "grunt", along with a wah pedal. In later years he also used a Japanese Fresher Straighter that to all intents and purposes was a Strat copy.

Phelps "Catfish" Collins was brother to the famous bassist Bootsie, and had a brief stint with Brown as part of the JB's from 1970-1971, when most of his original band quit over a pay dispute. This short period of time featured some of Brown's most intense and enduring recordings, including *Get Up (I Feel Like Being A Sex Machine), Super Bad* and *Give It Up Or Turn It Loose.* After breaking away from Brown, the Collins brothers went on to join George Clinton's Parliament-Funkadelic collective (which we'll explore in Chapter Seven).

Collins used a number of guitars over the years, including Fender Strat and Jazzmaster models. During his early work with James Brown and Funkadelic he used a Vox Ultrasonic guitar, notable by its in-built effects (including a palm-operated Wah Wah behind the bridge). Although he can be heard on a string of great singles (that appeared to be live but had overdubbed applause), his sound and playing are best defined on the astounding *Love Power Peace: Live at the Olympia* from 1971. The sound is classic clean Fender Silverface/Blackface, cranked to slight breakup (although it's possible Collins engages the Vox's in-built distortion at points during the concert too).

Hearlon "Cheese" Martin joined the JB's from 1970-1975 and featured on some of Brown's most memorable albums including *Hotpants, Get on the Good Foot* and *The Payback*. His style managed to encapsulate much of the great work by Nolen and Collins (particularly as he played with both guitarists live), and far from playing second fiddle to either, he was largely responsible for one of the most defining rhythms that has dominated Funk for the last 50 years.

Martin was always conspicuous by his cream-white Telecaster, normally with the warmer neck pickup selected, probably playing through some kind of Fender amp.

Further Listening:

Papa's Got a Brand New Bag

Give It Up or Turn It Loose

Super Bad

Funky Drummer

Get on The Good Foot

Soul Power

The Payback

Jimmy Nolen

If James Brown was the Godfather of Soul, Jimmy Nolen was certainly the Godfather of Funk Guitar, pioneering so many of the techniques and sounds we take for granted now. Our first example features some crossover with RnB/Soul with sliding Steve Cropper-style major 6ths alongside Jimmy's early forays into *chicken scratch*. It's in the horn-friendly key of Eb (like many of Brown's early recordings) and wouldn't be complete without the ubiquitous dominant 9 chords.

Schooled in RnB and Jazz, Jimmy often favoured smaller chord fragments as you can see here. Under the fingers this looks like a Gm7(b5) and is played with the first and second (barred) fingers:

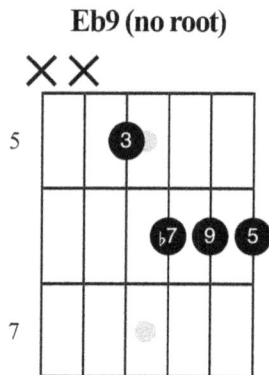

Eb9 (no root)

As you'll see in bar two, Jimmy's single note ideas tended to be based around the chord and he often used simple octaves, b7 and minor/major 3rd ideas rather than scalic shapes. If you want to see the wider picture, these notes are based around the Eb Mixolydian scale, with the minor 3rd (Gb) used as a passing note.

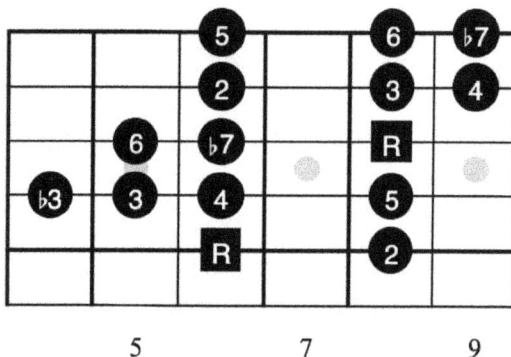

In this first groove you'll hear some common Funk devices: syncopation and fretting hand muting. This is combined with Jimmy's unique method of picking close to the bridge. There's much more tension in the strings at the bridge, so it creates a slightly thinner, more percussive/punchy sound.

Remember to download all the audio examples and backing tracks at **www.fundamental-changes.com**. All of the examples in this book have full backing tracks.

Example 1a

Keep your fretting hand soft throughout, as this will help mute the unwanted strings while providing the required percussive sound (even on the fretted notes). Use your spare fingers to mute unwanted open strings so you don't have to adjust your picking hand technique for the single notes (i.e., maintain a smooth 1/16th note alternate motion throughout).

The next groove is a great example of Nolen's relentless 1/16th note technique, all focused on swung single notes. It can take some time to build up to his almost superhuman stamina, so take this slowly at first. Be mindful of any tension that can easily creep into your forearm or shoulder.

Example 1b

A trademark of much of James Brown's Funk career was moving to the IV for the bridge section. This signature move has become almost synonymous with Funk, and in the next example we see this idea used with classic dominant 9 and 13 extensions (something Catfish Collins used to great effect in *Sex Machine* a few years after Nolen). We're in the key of Eb, so the IV chord is Ab and the V will be Bb. The move to the V chord creates the anticipation of returning to the I chord.

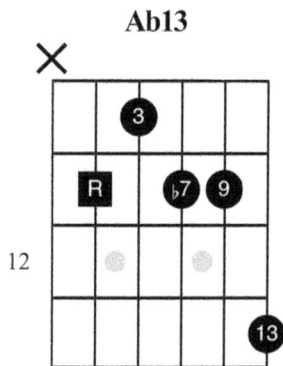

Ab13

Example 1c

The emphasis here is on the offbeat 1/16th note upstrokes that create the syncopation against the classic Clyde Stubblefield-style drum groove. As with the previous examples, a light touch with the fretting hand will do wonders to create a choppier, more percussive sound. The semitone chord slides also became something of a Nolen trademark, that all subsequent guitarists with James Brown then followed.

The next two ideas are a great example of how Nolen and fellow guitarist Alphonso "Country" Kellum would find parts that fit together seamlessly without stepping on each other's toes. The initial descending Bb Minor Pentatonic idea is split across two guitars in two octaves as in *I Feel Good*, with the main groove featuring Nolen's usual single note picking, this time based loosely upon an early cover favourite called *The Chicken*.

Example 1d

Kellum's job was to largely to stay out of the way of Nolen's intricate 1/16th note ideas, so in the example below we see economy of movement and space on the 2 and 4 beats. Since Nolen is filling much of the bar, it's important to pay attention to these rests, as they're crucial to create space between the two parts. Another key aspect to consider when writing funk parts for two guitars is the use of different registers. The parts are played at opposite ends of the neck in these examples, which creates further separation in both pitch and timbre.

Example 1e

The next riff draws on the hypnotic groove of *Funky Drummer* with what looks like a fragment of this typical blues shape:

G9 (no root)

The underlying harmony in the example is minor but the small triangular shape inside this chord (b7, 9, 5) contains no 3rd, which means it can loosely function either as a dominant 9 or minor 9 chord. The fifth string can sound a bit full and muddy, so partial two and three note chords like this are much more effective in keeping a "chanky" Funk sound.

Example 1f

The temptation in the example above is to strum through the whole riff with constant "chukka chukka" 1/16th note mutes, but the three precise string mutes on beat 1 are an essential part of the Nolen chicken scratch style. Take note that your picking hand will constantly switch between single and multi-string mutes. Developing an awareness of how and where your pick hits the strings is one of the key lessons here.

Phelps "Catfsh" Collins

Our next groove is a great example of Collins' energetic 1/16th note playing, as heard on tracks such as *Super Bad*. Collins' ferocious picking hand is relentless at higher tempos, so maintaining a good floating hand position and a very loose wrist in the picking hand is essential to success. If the pick digs into the strings at all, you'll stumble. Try not to aim into the body of the guitar on the downstroke (i.e., your pick shouldn't travel into the pickguard). Keep a close eye on any tension creeping into your forearm or shoulder.

Example 1g

The next example is based upon Collins' most famous riff from his short stint with the JB's: *Sex Machine*. It also combines one of his trademark pull-off lines, possibly inspired by the legato riffs played by Brown's incredible horn section.

Example 1h

We're normally taught to avoid pull-offs from the major to minor 3rd in blues, but it works here, as the predominant sound still heard is the D7 chord. This is also a nice coordination exercise, as it should be approached with downstrokes, with the pull-off manoeuvre happening as the picking hand returns in mid-air as an upstroke.

Our next example demonstrates some of Collins' jazz roots with a riff based around D Dorian with some chromatic octaves thrown in for good measure. Check out his extended solo on the 1971 Paris Olympia live rendition of *Sex Machine* where you'll hear his amazing Wes Montgomery-meets-Funk style in all its glory. Here we're using D Dorian with some passing bluesy b5 notes to fill in some of the gaps:

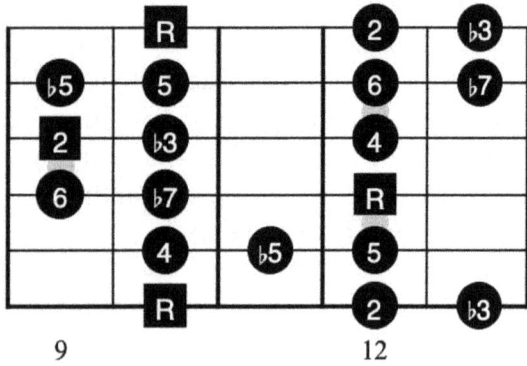

Try to visualise and target the Dorian-specific major 6th interval inside this scale, as it's this note that gives the minor-sounding scale its slightly brighter, jazzier sound.

Example 1i

The jazzier sound of this groove is further enhanced by the rootless Dm9 in bar two. This chord is another super useful chord shape that crops up time and again in Funk as it also doubles as an alternative major 7 shape:

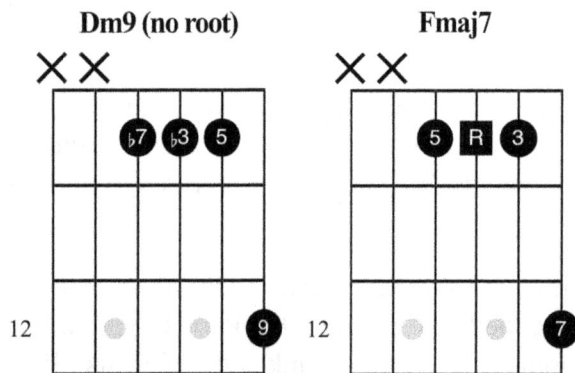

Hearlon "Cheese" Martin

The next rhythmic idea is arguably one of the most important in Funk and one that you'll hear repeated time and again. It can be viewed as a development of the Latin *Tresillo* or *Rumba Rhythm* that is heard all over Latin America and in a lot of RnB and pop music:

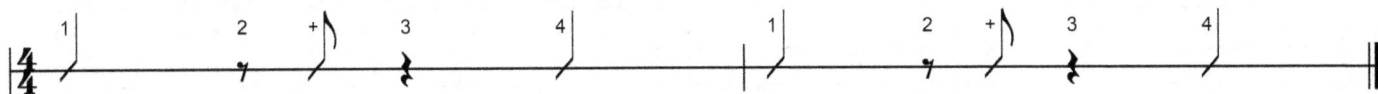

Counting "1 2 3 1 2 3 1 2" with the emphasis on the "1" is a great way to really feel this rhythm at first. The identifiable 3/3/2 grouping can be heard in tracks such as *Stone to the Bone* and leads to a sort of *double tresillo* in Hearlon Martin classics such as *The Payback*, *Hotpants* and *Make it Funky*.

The 3/3/3/3/2/2 grouping heard in these tracks can be strummed/counted as follows (note the switch of picking direction on every "1" where you should feel the accent):

1   2   3   1   2   3   1   2   3   1   2   3   1   2   1   2

This idea creates a lot of cross-rhythms and syncopation, and can be seen in the next example where the picking hand follows these groupings of three 1/16th notes. Beat four is effectively used as a pivot in the bar to get back to the downbeat on beat 1, so experiment with different rhythmic combinations here.

There are two backing tracks for this example to help you practice and experiment with both straight and swung rhythms. James Brown and many other Funk artists play around with the strength of the swing, so it pays to zone in on the other instruments in the band to help lock in with the rhythmic grid. In this case, the tambourine can really help since it's playing a constant 1/16th note rhythm.

Example 1j

Eb9 ... E9

```
T|--6-X-X-6-X-X-6-X-X-6-X-X-6-6-X-X----6-X-X-6-X-X-6-X-X-6-X-X-6-X-X----7-7-X-X--
 |--6-X-X-6-X-X-6-X-X-6-X-X-6-6-X-X----6-X-X-6-X-X-6-X-X-6-X-X-6-X-X----7-7-X-X--
A|--6-X-X-6-X-X-6-X-X-6-X-X-6-6-X-X----6-X-X-6-X-X-6-X-X-6-X-X-6-X-X----7-7-X-X--
 |--5-X-X-5-X-X-5-X-X-5-X-X-5-5-X-X----5-X-X-5-X-X-5-X-X-5-X-X-5-X-X----6-6-X-X--
B|--6-X-X-6-X-X-6-X-X-6-X-X-6-6-X-X----6-X-X-6-X-X-6-X-X-6-X-X-6-X-X----7-7-X-X--
```

Eb9 ... E9

```
T|--6-X-X-6-X-X-6-X-X-6-X-X-6-6-X-X----6-X-X-6-X-X-6-X-X-6-X-X-6-X-X----7----7--
 |--6-X-X-6-X-X-6-X-X-6-X-X-6-6-X-X----6-X-X-6-X-X-6-X-X-6-X-X-6-X-X----7----7--
A|--6-X-X-6-X-X-6-X-X-6-X-X-6-6-X-X----6-X-X-6-X-X-6-X-X-6-X-X-6-X-X----7----7--
 |--5-X-X-5-X-X-5-X-X-5-X-X-5-5-X-X----5-X-X-5-X-X-5-X-X-5-X-X-5-X-X----6----6--
B|--6-X-X-6-X-X-6-X-X-6-X-X-6-6-X-X----6-X-X-6-X-X-6-X-X-6-X-X-6-X-X----7----7--
```

The next groove is a slight variation of the previous example and focuses on the more economical tritone (b5) shape. Depending on how you look at these two intervals, they could either be viewed as the 3rd and b7 (G and Db) of Eb dominant 7 or the b7 and 3rd (G and C#) of A dominant 7 – a very useful shape in Funk!

Example 1k

Eb9 ... 4x

```
T|--6-X-X-6-X-X-6-6-X-6-X-X-6-X-X-X----6-X-X-6-X-X-6-X-X-6-X-X-6-6-X-X--
A|--5-X-X-5-X-X-5-5-X-5-X-X-5-X-X-X----5-X-X-5-X-X-5-X-X-5-X-X-5-5-X-X--
```

Our final riff on the whistle-stop tour of James Brown-style Funk is an homage to the 12/8 groove heard in *Doing it to Death*. Martin's choppy rhythm can be seen as a development of the cross-rhythm idea studied in the previous two examples, except here it's what is known as a *three over two* polyrhythm (three rhythms are heard against two counts). Although this is in 12/8, you'll feel it as triplets in 4/4. The basic idea can therefore be broken down into playing a note/chord on every other triplet 1/8th note as follows:

TRI – p – **LET**   tri – **P** – let   **TRI** – p – let   **TRI** – p – let

As you can see, explicit alternate strumming will give you accents on Down, Down, Down, Down, Up. In the next example you can see that this can be varied, and I've included some typical Cheese Martin pick directions to show you how. Strict alternate strumming would mean an upstroke on beat 4, which can feel a little awkward, but you should experiment to find the most natural feel with the picking hand.

Example 1l

The final example is a typical Jimmy Nolen style accompaniment to the previous riff and fits neatly in the cracks. When you get this right, there'll be a satisfying yo-yo effect between the two guitars. This is a great exercise in focus and rhythmic interplay, although be wary of getting drawn towards the other rhythm.

Example 1m

Chapter Two – Swamp Funk: The New Orleans Connection

The players: Leo Nocentelli

Chapter Overview: Son and New Orleans Clave, using diatonic 3rds and 6ths, Mixolydian chords.

It's possible to trace the DNA of Funk back to the melting pot of Jazz and the funeral marching bands of the early 1900s in New Orleans, Louisiana. Marching band drummers play a syncopated style that is commonly referred to as *Second Line,* whereby improvised marching-style beats and polyrhythms are played in and around Afro-Cuban and Caribbean-influenced rhythms. The *NOLA funk backbeat* adapted this rhythmic blueprint and can be heard in any number of '50s RnB and Rock 'n' Roll tracks, popularised by artists such as Fats Domino and Professor Longhair. James Brown himself adapted the second line rhythms taught to him by two New Orleans-schooled drummers for his brand of Funk. This effectively came full circle when local bands started to integrate his ideas with hometown influences. This combination of styles found its swampy, funky zenith in bands such as The Meters, the Neville Brothers and Dr John.

Leo Nocentelli is arguably the most important guitarist in this style. He grew up in New Orleans and wrote some of the most iconic hits of The Meters, including *Cissy Strut, Chicken Strut* and *Hey Pocky A-Way.* Simplicity, improvisation and an often greasy, swampy, swinging groove are at the forefront of Nocentelli's style. As well as influencing a whole generation of guitar players with the Meters, he also went on to become a very successful session guitarist, working with the likes of Dr John, Robert Palmer, Etta James, Joe Cocker and Albert King.

Nocentelli has long favoured his black 1976 Fender Starcaster (Fender's short foray into the semi hollow body market) but used a Telecaster on all the early Meters material. He recently switched to a Gibson ES-335 citing its greater versatility, although you won't quite get the same "spank" and response in the picking hand as a Fender. Amp-wise, Nocentelli originally used Fenders (probably a Twin or Deluxe), although these days he uses Mesa-Boogie. More important than the guitar/amp combination, however, is having a good clean, core sound with a healthy amount of reverb.

Further Listening:

Cissy Strut

Look A Py-Py

Just Kissed My Baby

Hey Pocky A-Way

Fire on The Bayou

Leo Nocentelli

The 3-2 Son Clave (and the 2-3 Son Clave) are fundamental rhythmic elements in Afro-Cuban music. In simple terms, these are two bar rhythms that have a "2 side" and a "3 side" meaning two rhythms in one of the bars, and three rhythms in the other. Notice that the three side is exactly the same as the *Tresillo* pattern we looked at with Hearlon Martin's grooves in the previous chapter.

Having a grasp of the 3-2 Son Clave shown above (often known as the Bo Diddley beat), is fundamental in understanding how this was applied to music from New Orleans. This is mirrored in our first Meters-style groove, that can be viewed as a sort of New Orleans variation of the Son Clave.

Example 2a

A wide, laid-back swing and soft fretting hand is key to reproducing the sound and feel of The Meters' typical "between-the-cracks" style of second line Funk. Notice that the displaced 1/16th note beat on the "e" of beat 4 adds a natural upstroke, creating a little more syncopation than the standard Son Clave. The second part is a natural Nocentelli variation with an extra double strum on the "&" of beat 2, but you should experiment with moving this placement around the bar to come up with your own lines.

The next groove really sums up some of the main stylistic traits of Leo Nocentelli: a simple G Minor Pentatonic riff doubled by the bass and interspersed with small chord fragments. Unlike much of the constant 1/16th note strumming approach of Chapter One, this means more attention is needed in your picking hand. Adjust the height of the arm depending on which strings you need to concentrate on (e.g., a lower position for the double stop on beats 3 and 4 to avoid the unwanted open strings). It can be helpful to think of these as separate ideas initially, so you could practice them in isolation (e.g., just the pentatonic riff, resting for the chords).

Example 2b

The next riff combines some nice 3rd and 6th chord ideas, with the b7 (Bb) providing a dominant 7, C Mixolydian sound.

Example 2c

It's a hugely worthwhile exercise mapping and learning your diatonic 3rds and 6ths up and down the fretboard with a sideways "lateral" approach. This means you can stick to two-string sets and this will help you visualise the natural pattern. It's also great for adding colour and interest to standard chordal lines.

Here are C Mixolydian 3rds on the third and fourth string to get you started:

3 5 7 9 12

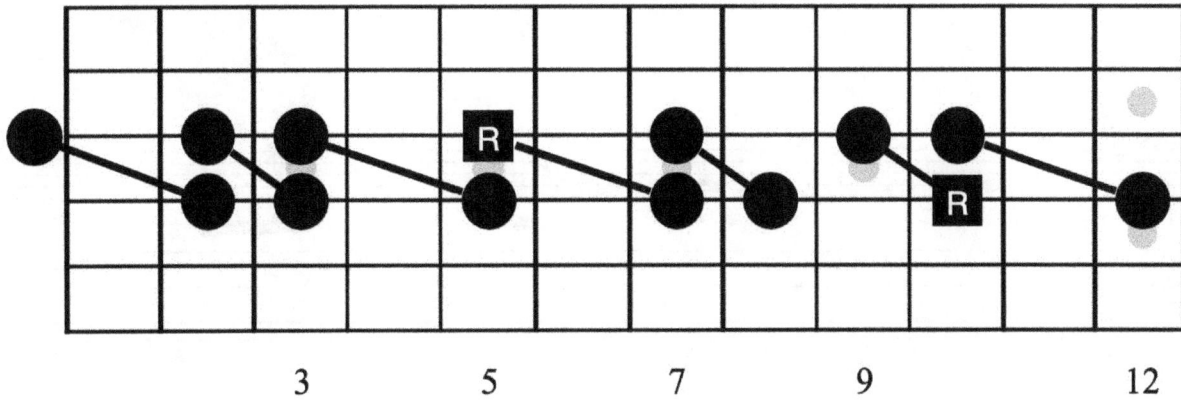

The next groove is a good lesson in creating multiple variations of the same chord (Dm in this case). The latter half of the bar can be viewed as the response to the power chord idea, so these riffs/licks can be easily interchanged or varied.

Example 2d

The final groove starts with a relatively simple arpeggiated idea, but the swing and crossing of strings make it a great alternate picking exercise too. The second bar is a typical modal jazz/blues approach to comping, using chords that are diatonic to A Mixolydian.

Example 2e

Chapter Three – 1970s RnB Funk

The players: Leroy "Sugarfoot" Bonner, Tony Maiden, Steve Cropper, Hamish Stuart/Onnie McIntyre, Bruce Conte.

Chapter Overview: Rhythmic displacement and syncopation, the 1/16th note push, using the tritone, extended chords, using chromatic "outside" notes.

The profound shift from Soul and RnB into Funk during the 1970s saw many bands take up the mantle of James Brown's innovations during the previous decade. Funk itself is, of course, a blend of many different genres including RnB, and all of the following guitarists were skilled in crossing these genres.

Leroy "Sugarfoot" Bonner is one of the most underrated Funk guitarists in our entire list. He was the guitarist and lead singer of a group called the Ohio Players, who reached peak funkiness and success during the 1970s with such hits as *Love Rollercoaster* (later covered by the Red Hot Chilli Peppers), *Funky Worm* and *Fire*. Their style was highly eclectic, fusing together RnB, Funk, Soul and Jazz with a raucous Rock sensibility and a slick presentation (and risqué album covers!) At the heart of Bonner's extrovert double-necked presentation was a style steeped in Blues, yet it is his ability to nail down some of the dirtiest Funk grooves that makes him stand out here.

Bonner was instantly recognisable by his double-neck Mosrite guitar (12 and 6 string necks) a Californian brand that was popular from the 1950s all the way through to the 1990s. The guitar featured high output humbucking pickups and very thin, narrow necks. He used an Acoustic model 271 head and cab, famous for its high output and white "police siren" horn in the cab section.

Tony Maiden is another unsung hero from the world of Funk, featuring on classic Rufus and Chaka Khan albums between 1974-1983. He might not be a household name, but the mere mention of tracks such as *Tell Me Something Good, Once You Get Started* and *Ain't Nobody* should easily cement his position in our hall of fame. Maiden joined the band in mid-1974 and went on to record and compose on some seminal Funk albums including *Rufusized, Rufus featuring Chaka Khan* and *Ask Rufus*. He had a sublime sense of playing "in the pocket" and an ability to fuse chord melody with RnB lines, along with a real understanding of space and part-writing. Although he was no slouch when it came to soloing, his vocals were also outstanding, and he would, incredibly go toe-to-toe with Chaka.

Although Maiden is well-known for using a talk box to solo on *Tell Me Something Good*, like many of our funkateers his core rhythm sound came from playing through Fender Twin amps. The old adage that it's "all in the fingers" perhaps has a ring of truth, as he played a wide variety of guitars from the Gibson ES-175 and Les Pauls to a Fender Mustang.

Hamish Stuart was singer/guitarist and frontman of the Average White Band between 1972 and 1982 and went on to work with Soul/Funk giants Aretha Franklin and Chaka Khan, as well as artists as diverse as David Sanborn, George Benson and Paul McCartney. Onnie McIntyre was another founding member and fellow rhythm guitarist alongside Stuart, and their relatively simple guitar parts were straight out of the James Brown philosophy of part writing. Although a band hailing from Scotland might seem a bit incongruous here, Funk hits such as *Pick Up The Pieces* and their seminal albums *AWB* and *Cut The Cake* inspired the J.B.'s (James Brown's backing band) to write *Pick Up The Pieces, One By One* under the name AABB (Above Average Black Band) in a tongue in cheek homage to their Funk credentials.

Stuart is probably best known for his cherry red 1967 Epiphone Casino, used on Chaka Khan's first three albums (it's the guitar on *I'm Every Woman*) and with Paul McCartney from 1987-1993. It even appears on the later-years AWB hit *Let's Go Round Again*. In early AWB, when Stuart wasn't playing bass, he'd use everything from Fender Strats and Teles to a White Gretsch, whilst McIntyre was always a Strat man throughout the AWB years. Both usually played through Fender Twins.

Steve "The Colonel" Cropper is an absolute giant in the guitar world. He's perhaps best known for his work with the legendary Stax house band, Booker T. and the M.G.'s, who backed the likes of Otis Redding, Wilson Pickett, Sam and Dave, Bill Withers and Albert King. While Cropper isn't thought of as an out and out Funk guitarist, his economical rhythm playing can be seen as the starting point for a lot of Funk, and tracks such as *Soul Man* and *Sookie Sookie* by Don Covay bear this out. It's on the album *Melting Pot* by Booker T that Cropper's Funk prowess really comes to the fore, however.

Cropper's main guitar for years was a White '62 or '63 Telecaster with a rosewood fingerboard. During most of the Stax sessions he played through either a Fender Harvard or Super Reverb amp that can be heard on all the iconic recordings such as *Dock of The Bay* and *Soul Man*.

Bruce Conte was a member of Oakland uber-Funk outfit Tower of Power between 1972-1979. They were known for their super-tight horn section and high-level musicianship that spawned some classic Funk albums during the mid-70s. Although the horns inevitably took centre-stage, Conte's work on eight studio albums became very much part of the signature TOP sound, with his syncopated Funk grooves sitting alongside Jazz, Soul and Blues, as well as some stinging lead work. His fluid rhythmic style was a great fit for the greasy, gritty style of the band, personified by such classics as *What Is Hip* and *Squib Cakes*. He also wrote two of the band's best slow soul ballads, *Just Another Day* and *Love's Been Gone So Long*.

Throughout his entire tenure with TOP, Conte used a beautiful 1957 Les Paul Goldtop through a 1967 Blackface Super Reverb. He also occasionally used Vox Wah Wah and MXR Phase 90 pedals.

Further Listening:

(Leroy Bonner)

Food Stamps Y'All – The Ohio Players

Skin Tight – The Ohio Players

Love Rollercoaster – The Ohio Players

(Tony Maiden)

Tell Me Something Good – Rufus & Chaka Khan

Rufusized – Rufus & Chaka Khan

I'm A Woman – Rufus & Chaka Khan

(Steve Cropper)

Soul Man – Sam and Dave

Chicken Pox – Booker T. & the M.G.'s

Melting Pot – Booker T. & the M.G.'s

(Hamish Stuart/Onnie McIntyre)

Pick Up the Pieces – Average White Band

Person to Person – Average White Band

Work to Do – Average White Band

(Bruce Conte)

What Is Hip? – Tower of Power

Down to The Nightclub – Tower of Power

Squib Cakes – Tower of Power

Leroy "Sugarfoot" Bonner

Although Bonner was really fond of layering multiple guitar parts, he kept things simple and efficient when there were horns, keys and other guitars in the band. The secret sauce here is finding space rhythmically and sonically to avoid fighting with the other instruments. All these examples use some common Bonner traits including staccato rhythms and repetition of similar intervals. For the staccato picking, return the pick to lightly mute the string you've just played (don't use your fretting hand).

Example 3a

In the next groove, Bonner's mix of syncopated rhythm and lead ideas provides a refreshing take on Funk guitar. The opening sliding E9 idea should be recognisable from the earlier James Brown chapter, but the use of diatonic 3rds is pure Soul/RnB. These 3rds also use a great *rhythmic displacement* idea whereby the group of three diads are displaced/moved along by one 1/16th note each time they're played. Also take note of the tritone shape on beat 3 bar two, targeting major 6th and minor 3rd notes. This is a great Funk cliché that sounds great all over the neck.

Example 3b

The next groove targets the b7 and 6th and features the same cliché lick as the previous example (this time from G Mixolydian rather than E Mixolydian). The riff is the first of an interlocking two-part line and is very straight, with most of the rhythms landing on either strong downbeats or offbeat 1/8th notes. The inherent funkiness of this line really comes from its relationship with the second guitar.

Example 3c

The second guitar is typical of the dirtier Rock tones Bonner was known for. The rhythms are more heavily syncopated and broken up with plenty of space, providing a call and response effect between guitar 1 and 2. The 1/16th note *push* is a feature that crept into a lot of 1970s Funk (the last 1/16th note of the bar is *pushed* into a tied downbeat) and is in abundance here. This can be a notoriously tricky rhythm to feel correctly, however. A great way to approach this is to play a muted downstroke on the & of beat 4 (where the rest is marked) allowing for a more precise upstroke on the pushed 1/16th.

Example 3d

Although both riffs are technically based around G Dorian, it can be better to think of the note pool simply as G Minor Pentatonic with an added major 6th. Viewing it this way can have the added benefit of helping your improvised ideas sound less scalic in nature.

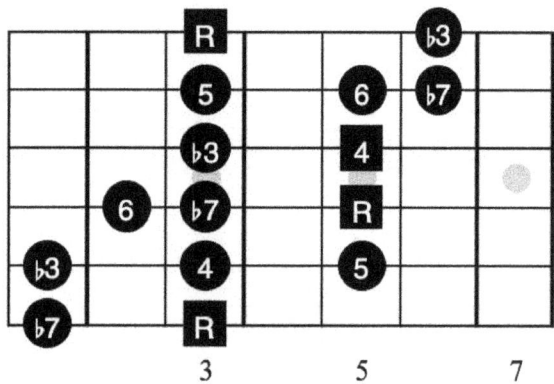

The next riffs go together on the sort of slow groove that was sampled so much by rap in the '80s. There's a bit of swing, so try to lock in with the clavinet and bass guitar parts that will help guide you. The first example sticks to G Minor Pentatonic, while the second once again targets the 6th and b7 from the G Dorian scale.

Example 3e

Example 3f

Tony Maiden

This first groove shows Maiden's penchant for mixing Funk and Blues vocabulary, with some typical diad (two note chord) licks in and around G Blues/G Mixolydian. A lot of his improvisation over dominant chords combines this chordal/single note approach, so it's worth ensuring you're familiar with both scales and how they can be superimposed over one another. Here, the G Mixolydian scale relates directly to the underlying G7 harmony, while the Blues scale is used for hip passing notes such as the b3 and b5.

G Mixolydian / G Blues

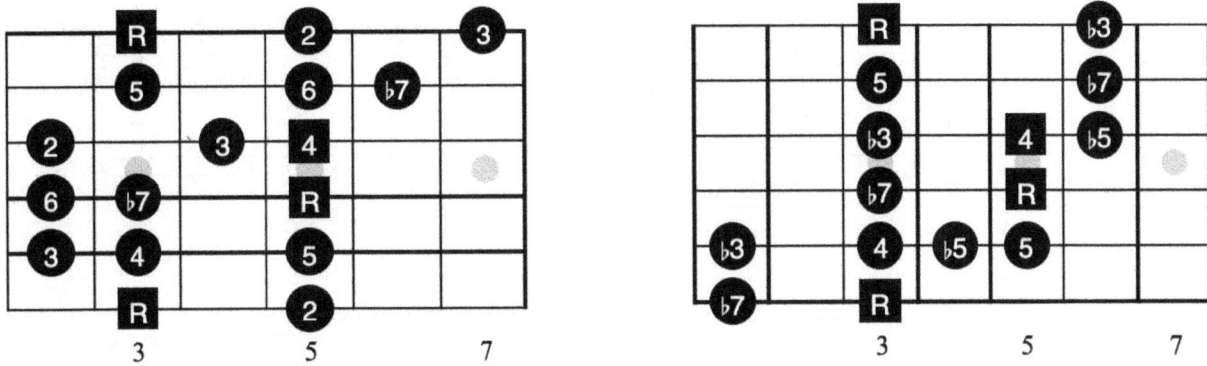

Exercise 3g

The next riff sees a typical Rufus move from I to IV (G7 to C7), targeting the funky tritone shape that we saw in the first chapter with Hearlon Martin (the E and Bb are the 3rd and b7 from C7). Once again, there are some 1/16th note pushes at the end of bars one to three, so take care to ensure your foot doesn't follow this, hitting the downbeat instead.

The main technique focus should be on constant 1/16th note motion over several strings, with a much wider strumming arc in the picking hand. There needs to be excellent muting in the fretting hand, so a flatter hand/finger shape and using any spare fingers to mute the unwanted open strings will really help with this.

Exercise 3h

Maiden also had a rockier side, with muscular distorted riffs providing a contrast to cleaner lines. This idea uses the E Blues scale with added major 6th (C#), which can feel a little strange, as standard E Blues-Rock riffs tend to favour the first and third fingers. The pull-off in bar two, for example, needs to be executed with the fourth and second fingers to allow the first finger to fret the 4th fret C#.

Example 3i

Next is the counterpoint lead melodic line. Notice how this idea primarily uses the brighter E Major Pentatonic scale (another typical Blues trick) as a contrast to the mostly minor-sounding previous riff. The trick to making this sound good is to not explicitly play the major 3rd (G#), so be careful not to overcook your bends from the 11th fret (F#).

Example 3j

33

The final Tony Maiden-style riff shows more of his Pop/Soul/Jazz side, so here you'll immediately notice a more sophisticated approach to harmony. The C7alt is a jazzy variation on the V7 chord that crept into a lot of Funk as the '70s progressed. The *alt* refers to altered 5th/9th intervals that are either augmented (raised a semitone) or diminished (lowered a semitone). In the case of the chord used here, its full spelling is C7(#5 #9).

Example 3k

Steve Cropper

This first groove is a spin on the classic Sam & Dave track *Soul Man*. Although Cropper wasn't typically renowned for classic Funk chords like the dominant 9, he did favour partial shapes such as these basic root position and 1st/2nd inversion chords. Each of them requires careful *stubbing* of the third finger against the open fifth string (the fleshy pad frets the fourth string while the tip touches the adjacent string enough to mute it) and a slight angle of attack is needed from the picking hand to avoid the bottom two strings entirely.

Example 3l

The next idea focuses on a lovely partial shape (3rd fret G and 6th fret F) that produces a "crunchy" close interval voicing that we'll see Prince use extensively later in this book. These two notes are the root and b7, so are equally useful for dominant and minor 7 chords. These are interspersed with jazzier Dorian chords (the E natural in the C/G is the major 6th from G Dorian).

Example 3m

In the next groove there's a passing resemblance to Hendrix but perhaps that's down to the E7(#9) and pentatonic nature of the riff rather than anything else. It's classic instrumental Booker T territory, however, with the clean E Minor Pentatonic scale snaking around syncopated chords and the added swing that creates an instant Funk feel.

Example 3n

It's worth noting that the erroneously named *Hendrix chord* effectively contains both major and minor 3rds (the #9 is the equivalent of a minor 3rd interval). This creates an interesting ambiguity within the chord that means it's neither major nor minor. This split personality is great, as it can slot into most bluesy/funky chord progressions, either as a static I chord or as a V chord in either major or minor keys.

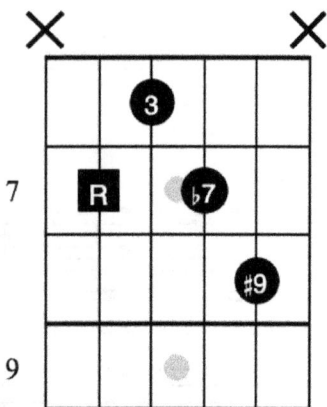

Hamish Stuart/Onnie McIntyre

The first Average White Band-style groove demonstrates the band's great ability to create interlocking parts. Although we explored the concept of individual parts existing in their own pocket of space with James Brown, AWB had a great way of combining chordal Funk rhythm with more melodic single note lines. The first example is a typical McIntyre groove that focuses on a diad shape comprising A (4th) and D (b7th) giving a slightly ambiguous suspended sound (there's no 3rd in this chord, so E7sus4 is the harmony implied by both guitar parts combined).

Example 3o

This allows room for the more melodic Hamish Stuart idea in the next example, based around E Mixolydian. The minor to major 3rd (G to G#) is a typical Blues move that instantly gives a hipper sound as it resolves to the major 3rd from an *outside* note a semitone below. This is a neat trick that you could try on literally any consonant *inside* note, although you need to use it sparingly.

Example 3p

The next example takes this "resolve up a semitone" trick a step further with small chord fragments from A Mixolydian.

If you're following this book in order, the Funk/Blues diad ideas should be recognisable from some of Tony Maiden's grooves.

Example 3q

We're referring to the final chord as a G/A rather than Gadd9 since the bass guitar and overall harmony mean the key centre/root is A. This is sometimes referred to as A9sus or even A11, as it sounds like a dominant chord (even though there's no 3rd). It's a massively useful chord, as you'll see in the Disco Funk chapter later on.

The final example is another Hamish Stuart-style groove that fits alongside the previous example. It uses rhythmically and technically complex single notes with palm-muting, so it's a great alternate picking precision exercise. It uses A Mixolydian as the framework with some outside chromatic passing notes to add extra flavour.

Example 3r

Bruce Conte

Conte was a huge Jimmy Nolen fan and this comes through in his frequent use of dominant 9 chords. Rather than stick to the James Brown static chord idea, Conte often moves his chords around chromatically. He also has a touch more harmonic sophistication and syncopation than JB-style Funk. This can be seen in the jazzy B7(#5 #9) chord that should be viewed as a V chord in the key of E.

Example 3s

The next groove follows a standard James Brown style I – IV chord movement, but here the same modal approach we looked at in Example 2e is used to add interest to the B7 chord. Many of Conte's grooves use this Jazz/Blues cliché, so it's worth exploring how it might fit over dominant chords in different keys and contexts.

Example 3t

The next groove is in Eb Major, but the chords aren't strictly diatonic. Some subtle alterations are used to add colour and interest. The Eb9, for example, *pulls* the ear to the Abmaj7 chord, as Eb9 acts like a V chord resolving to Abmaj7. Db9 – Ebmaj7 is known as a bVII – I chord progression in Roman numerals and is a common trick (known as a *backdoor cadence*) used as an alternative to the standard V – I perfect cadence

Example 3u

Conte's jazzier approach is even more evident in the final example, using *quartal harmony* (we'll cover this concept in detail in the Pop Funk chapter) to make up the minor 11 chords.

Example 3v

Chapter Four – Funk Soul

The players: Curtis Mayfield, Charles "Skip" Pitts, Sly/Freddie Stone, "Wah Wah" Watson, Ernie Isley.

Chapter overview: Creative wah techniques, E Minor Pentatonic pathways, "pat" technique.

Funk straddles many other styles of music, which often makes it difficult to see the line between them. This chapter can be categorised as the more laid-back, sexier side of Funk, and although the ubiquitous wah wah features prominently, the pace and energy of the music itself tends to be less frenetic.

The early 1970s saw many African American bands gain crossover success by moving from Motown and Soul into Funk. Many took a more experimental approach by blending Hendrix-style psychedelia with the essence of the James Brown ethos. This was also the time of so-called *Blaxploitation* movies that featured some amazing Funk Soul and Jazz soundtracks. Although this subgenre has a long and complicated history, the soundtracks from *Shaft* and *Superfly* are standouts from this period.

It's virtually impossible to talk about the soulful Funk of the '60s and '70s and not mention the slick production and playing of Curtis Mayfield. He's often seen as the main influence on Jimi Hendrix's soulful rhythm style (listen side-by-side to Mayfield's *People Get Ready* and Hendrix tracks such as *Castles Made of Sand* and *Have You Ever Been To (Electric Ladyland)* and it's as clear as day). Mayfield will largely be remembered for his stellar work on *Superfly,* however.

Mayfield was self-taught which led to him using an open F# tuning was inspired by the black keys on a piano: F# – A – C# – F# – A – F#. This inevitably led his guitar playing down a unique path, informing licks that are notoriously difficult to emulate from live footage. He played fingerstyle, with a combination of thumb and fingers, and was seen sporting a Fender Telecaster Thinline and '70s Stratocasters, usually set to the middle pickup position through Fender Twin amps.

The Isaac Hayes track *Theme from Shaft* is, in many people's minds, the quintessential wah-laden Funk track. Often erroneously credited to "Wah Wah" Watson, it was actually played by Charles "Skip" Pitts. As well as touring with Soul giants Wilson Pickett and Sam & Dave, he also had a stint with the Isley Brothers (his is the scratchy funk riff on *It's Your Thing*). He'll forever be remembered for his wah sound on Isaac Haye's blaxploitation soundtrack, however (especially as he was sampled by everyone from Dr Dre, Snoop Dog to Massive Attack and the Beastie Boys).

For his early work with Stax, including *Shaft,* Pitts used black and sunburst Les Paul Customs through Sunn heads and amps alongside a Fender Twin. The wah part that came to define *Shaft* was accidental and courtesy of a Maestro Boomerang Wah that Pitts was apparently testing while tuning up. The rest, as they say, is history.

Sly & The Family Stone are an absolute giant in the world of Funk, mixing many seemingly disparate styles such as Rock, Funk and Soul into their own pioneering brand of "psychedelic soul". While the band will be remembered for hits such as *Dance to The Music, Thank You (Falettinme Be Mice Elf Agin)* and *Family Affair*, the 1973 album *Fresh* is widely recognised as one of the most seminal Funk albums of the early '70s. Its stripped back arrangements might not have gained the same commercial success, but Sly's first foray into using a drum machine alongside some classic Funk grooves was genuinely ahead of its time.

When Sly wasn't playing organ, he was often seen sporting Standard and Thinline Telecasters and he would mainly play with the thumb. His brother Freddie used hollow body Gibson L-4s and Fender Teles. In early live performances the band can be seen with a large backline of Fender Dual Showman amps and the ubiquitous Fender Twin.

Melvin Ragin, aka "Wah Wah" Watson was originally part of the legendary Detroit studio session outfit *The Funk Brothers* and laid the foundation for huge artists such as The Four Tops, The Supremes and Martha Reeves. It was during this time that he developed his iconic wah technique that went on to grace a huge number of tracks. The iconic intro to The Temptations' *Papa Was a Rolling Stone* features a wide number of his trademark sounds and, alongside the sexy wah intro to Marvin Gaye's classic *Let's Get It On,* Watson proved that the wah could be used for more than the usual "whacka whacka" it was known for. His incredible roster of A-list artists grew when he went on to work on Herbie Hancock's *Death Wish* movie soundtrack, that sparked two decades of collaboration on some of the most influential Jazz Funk albums of the '70s and early '80s.

Watson always played a Gibson L5 archtop guitar for warmer, slightly broken up cleans alongside a Maestro Echoplex delay and Maestro Boomerang Wah for his arsenal of sound effects. Amp-wise, he can be seen in early gigs with a Fender Twin and later with Marshall amps for the Headhunters live sessions.

Ernie Isley was part of one of Funk Soul's longest surviving bands, the Isley Brothers. Younger brother Ernie joined the band in 1973 alongside elder brother Marvin on bass and brother-in-law Chris Jasper on keys, helping to transform it from a vocal trio into a fully-fledged band. A decade of success saw a string of great albums such as *3+3, Between the Sheets* and *The Heat is On,* which spawned such hits as *Summer Breeze, That Lady, Fight The Power* and *For The Love of You.*

In the early '70s Isley introduced fuzz guitar to a whole generation of soul fans that hadn't really heard much in the way of Rock lead guitar apart from Hendrix and Carlos Santana. The track in question was *That Lady* where an Electro-Harmonix Big Muff was used in tandem with a swirling Maestro Phase Shifter through a Fender Twin. His clean rhythm sound was also surprisingly direct and dry, unlike many Soul guitarists who tended to use the reverb tank on the amp. His guitar was a 1971 Fender Strat, in the neck position for most of the rhythm sounds and bridge position for fuzz lead.

Further Listening:

Superfly – Curtis Mayfield

Pusherman – Curtis Mayfield

Kung Fu – Curtis Mayfield

Theme from "Shaft" – Isaac Hayes (Skip Pitts)

The Breakdown – Rufus Thomas (Skip Pitts)

Thank You (Falettinme Be Mice Elf Agin) – Sly & The Family Stone

Loose Booty – Sly & The Family Stone

Sing a Simple Song – Sly & The Family Stone

Papa Was a Rolling Stone – The Temptations (Wah Wah Watson)

Hang Up Your Hang Ups – Herbie Hancock (Wah Wah Watson)

Doin It – Herbie Hancock (Wah Wah Watson)

That Lady – The Isley Brothers

Sunshine (Go Away Today) – The Isley Brothers

Hope You Feel Better Love – The Isley Brothers

Footsteps in The Dark – The Isley Brothers

Curtis Mayfield/Skip Pitts

The next three examples all fit over a typical "blaxploitation" style backing track and loosely combine the style of Curtis Mayfield with Skip Pitts' work with Isaac Hayes. The first is a simple idea in F# Minor that doubles up the bassline. The palm-muting adds a percussiveness that will help your clean sound cut through the lower frequencies of the bass. There's plenty of space and syncopation here, so although tapping your foot is essential practice, it can also be helpful to count the "1 & 2 & 3 & 4 &" out loud as well.

Example 4a

Next, is a classic Skip Pitts idea with rocking wah pedal and full string mutes. The cross symbol above the stave denotes a closed wah (the toe is to the ground) while the circle is fully open (heel to the ground). This should mostly feel like you're tapping your foot in time, though note the gradual opening of the wah on beat 4 of the second bar.

Example 4b

Mayfield was no slouch when it came to soloing, and although this book is strictly based upon Funk rhythm, it would be a shame to miss out his basic approach to soloing over this groove. There are some great ideas in this short solo and Hayes often used the wah pedal to add a lyrical, deeply funky texture.

The fast up and down slides are a little like the famous B.B. King "zinger", but the wah adds a whole new dimension. Likewise, the pull-offs and classic sliding 4ths sound great with a simple 1/4 note rhythm on the wah. Finally, the bend up and bend down on the adjacent string is classic Hendrix territory.

Example 4c

Sly & Freddie Stone

Like many two-guitar Funk bands, Sly and Freddie's parts were designed around simplicity and space. The next two examples are based on how the two guitarists would approach part writing, finding space with tone, rhythm and pitch/register. The first is a typical Sly Stone riff based around a highly recognisable A Blues idea. The almost Claptonesque A6 and A7 chords are given a funky twist by the sliding dominant 7th chords, using string mutes and adding wah.

Example 4d

Sly's driving rhythm allows for Freddie's wah-soaked solo/riff idea in the next example. The B.B. King zinger slide features once again with the main lick based around A Major Pentatonic. The final bar is where we start to hear the wah pedal used more as a rhythmic device. Here the A7 chord is held while the wah carries the underlying 1/8th note rhythm.

Example 4e

The next groove combines a lower string E Minor Pentatonic riff with higher string diads. To compose riffs like this, it can be helpful to visualise the pertinent parts of the E Minor Pentatonic scale across the whole fretboard. Here you should be able to see a repeated three-note/two-note pathway that will allow very simple first and third finger fretting throughout:

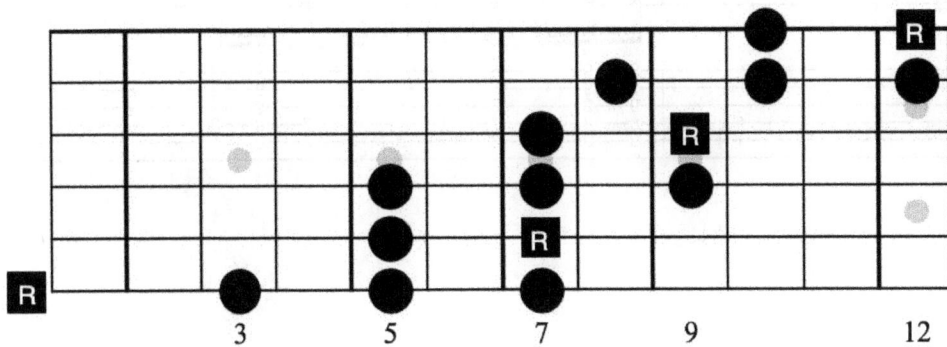

Example 4f

The final riff begins with a deceptively simple chromatic idea. Think of the C# on beat 2 as the target "inside" note (this is the 5th of the F# Major key). This idea of a target can be quite a useful approach when dealing with outside notes, as it helps the ear forgive the so-called "wrong" ones. It ends with one of Freddie's signature dominant 9 moves, though don't be tempted to slide between positions as this won't give you the same clarity as picking.

Example 4g

"Wah Wah" Watson

The first wah groove can really be seen as an extension of the classic "whacka whacka" sound that we saw with Skip Pitts and Curtis Mayfield. The G octave notes inside the fretting hand mutes are a nice coordination exercise between the two hands. The faster wah rhythm in bars two and four mean doubling your foot speed to 1/8th notes.

Example 4h

The next idea is one of Watson's favourite techniques that he used almost everywhere, on albums from Rose Royce to Blondie. The triplet rhythm needs a quick Down, Up, Down, finishing with an upstroke on beat 1 of the first bar. Use this final downbeat as the target for both the rhythm and the wah (go from open to closed).

Example 4i

The next concept is known in some circles as the *luxuriant swoon* and can best be described as a "sexy tremolo". Watson would usually have a delay of somewhere between 200-250ms with three or four repeats, then tremolo pick while the fretting hand slides from the pickup area down the fretboard. Think of those sultry sounds behind Barry White, Marvin Gaye and Maxwell and you'll instantly see how useful this simple technique can be.

Example 4j

The next groove uses Watson's gradual wah opening technique that creates a sort of mini crescendo. It's a great textural sound and can get you away from just rocking the wah on the main 1/4 note pulse. Since the wah will effectively be moving at different speeds, it can take some time to develop independence between the hands and the foot. You may even like to practice this without the guitar in hand.

Example 4k

The final example uses the *pat* technique that's probably better known as part of the slap bass arsenal. This is the technique of lightly patting the fretting hand fingers onto the string(s) to make a percussive sound, but without fretting any notes (it's best done with several flat fingers to avoid this). These can be played alongside normal fretting hand mutes for some interesting rhythmic combinations between the two hands.

Example 4l

Ernie Isley

Isley had a real penchant for the pick staccato technique we first looked at with Leroy Bonner. Here we're using the pick to immediately return to mute the previously picked note, rather than use the fretting hand to deaden the string.

Example 4m

Isley's frequent use of hammer-ons and pull-offs within simple chord shapes no doubt has Soul origins, but the speed and extra 1/16th note mutes in the next groove take us more into Funk territory.

Example 4n

No look at Ernie Isley would feel complete without a fuzz and phaser-drenched solo. You can use the backing track to blaze away in B Minor but integrating some key Isley ideas in your improvisation can be a lot of fun. The triplet hammer-on/pull-off idea is one of his go-to Blues-Rock ideas that borrows a lot from Clapton and Santana. This is varied slightly for the fiery repeated two-beat phrase in bars three and four. This is one of those occasions where breaking down the phrase into small parts (at least half tempo) can be beneficial. The hammer-on portion shouldn't be rushed and is a great lesson in legato/finger control and rhythmic discipline.

Example 4o

Chapter Five – Disco Funk

The players: Nile Rodgers, Claydes Charles Smith, Al McKay.

Chapter overview: Chord fragments, half-held chords, slash chords, improvising with octaves and 3rds, parallel mode "borrowed chords".

Disco largely developed during the thriving nightclub scene of late 1970s America, perhaps best represented by the infamous Studio 54 in Manhattan. The production of this music tended to be heavier and more costly, with lush string sections and shiny arrangements that were more complex than their earlier Funk counterparts.

One of the most iconic and influential Funk guitar players in this style is Nile Rodgers. Best known for his work with Chic and Sister Sledge, Nile's incredible career as a performer, producer and writer has seen him cumulatively sell over 100 million albums. The incredible roster of artists in his production back catalogue includes Madonna, Diana Ross, David Bowie, Daft Punk and Avicii. His style draws upon Jazz and RnB, with multi-layered lines that are put together with impeccable feel and timing.

Rodgers has famously used his "hitmaker" 1960 hardtail Stratocaster on everything, and apparently over $2 Billion worth of music has come from this one guitar alone. Unlike a lot of Funk players, who prefer the glassy out of phase sound between middle and neck pickup, Nile prefers to use the woodier, more open, rich neck single coil pickup. He also uses thin 0.5mm picks, preferring to add weight to his sound by having his thumb close to the edge of the pick. These picks tend to flap a little more than thicker picks, so the attack/transient on the strings feels and sounds completely different (anything below 1.0mm will get you surprisingly close). His sound is created either by going direct into a mixing console (as on tracks such as *Le Freak*) or direct and combined with a Fender amp (clean amps like a Twin, Princeton or Deluxe are perfect for this). If you want to get closer to his studio sound, Neve-style modelling in the form of the Neve 31102 Classic Console EQ can get you close, along with a touch of compression.

Claydes Charles Smith might not be a household name, but his work with the multiple platinum-selling Kool & the Gang saw the continuation and development of the James Brown school of part-writing mixed with a strong Jazz sensibility that drew on players such as Wes Montgomery and George Benson. His style uses octaves, syncopated single note lines and choppy partial chords to create the backbone to some of the most iconic songs that spanned early Funk all the way through to classic '70s Disco and '80s Pop.

Like a lot of funkateers, Smith was a lifelong Strat man, but like Leo Nocentelli of The Meters he was also known for using the short-lived Fender Starcaster (a bit like a Gibson ES-335) and occasionally Fender Teles. Like many of the Funk artists in this book, a neck single coil pickup into a clean Fender amp such as a Twin will get you close to his core sound. As his music and career progressed, Smith started to integrate effects such as chorus to accentuate the guitar's natural brightness (chorus is also great for capturing that '80s pop sound).

Al McKay was part of hit-making legends Earth, Wind & Fire, a band whose music spanned many different genres including RnB, Pop, Soul, Funk, Latin and, of course, Disco. McKay helped pen such classics as *September* and *Sing A Song,* as well as helping to write *Best of My Love* for the Emotions alongside Maurice White. His signature style is all about shiny, jangly Funk chords and overdubbed single note lines, together with a slightly more complex harmonic sensibility and a penchant for the use of effects such has a phaser, chorus and digital delay.

McKay was left-handed and mainly used a '72 Gibson ES-335 into a combination of Roland Jazz Chorus, Vox Super Beatle and Fender Twin Reverb amps. He also used a Roland Space Echo and several Boss effects including their Octaver, Chorus and Digital delay, but his personal favourite was the "chewy" sound of a phaser.

Further Listening:

(Nile Rogers)

Greatest Dancer – Chic

Good Times – Chic

Thinking of You – Sister Sledge

I'm Coming Out – Diana Ross

(Claydes Charles Smith)

Jungle Boogie – Kool & the Gang

Summer Madness – Kool & the Gang

Ladies Night – Kool & the Gang

Celebration – Kool & the Gang

(Al McKay)

Shining Star – Earth, Wind & Fire

Getaway – Earth, Wind & Fire

Jupiter – Earth, Wind & Fire

In The Stone – Earth, Wind & Fire

Nile Rodgers

In our first groove, minor 7 chords are given a simple tweak by the addition of sus4 ad libs. Nile often targets string zones (i.e., bottom, middle and top), so you'll rarely hear him play a succession of full six-string chords. This partial chord approach entails a more conscious and precise picking hand movement, but will give you more variation in your basic chord rhythms.

Example 5a

Also key to nailing Nile's chord sound is what I'd describe as the *half-held chord*. This involves releasing fretting hand pressure on the strings to somewhere between fully fretted and fully muted (Bruce Conte was also great at this). This takes a lot of practice to perfect, as you'll feel the urge to always press down fully (as we're taught to do) rather than let go slightly. Perfecting this technique will greatly add to your Funk playing, however, helping to produce a natural percussive sound that can be varied depending on the mood.

The next example is a throwback to the single note lines of Jimmy Nolen with some Rodgers twists (listen to the intro to the Sister Sledge classic *He's The Greatest Dancer* to hear this technique in action). Nile's technique uses palm-muting, together with relentless 1/16th note movement in the picking hand. It also uses a number of ghost notes on the open D string that are improvised in between the full mutes. Try to think of these as quiet, unaccented notes, as we don't really want to hear the open D with an obvious picked sound.

Example 5b

Key to success here is maintaining constant movement in the picking hand, with the motion coming from the wrist (not the thumb joint). Remember to unaccent the non-fretted notes (all the open string ghost notes and fretting hand mutes) with a little more "snap" on the fretted notes.

The next groove is a masterclass in simple chords, belying some complex background harmony that's being played by piano and bass. Nile spends much of his time playing these smaller chord fragments without the need to explicitly spell out the full chord. It sounds a lot cleaner and funkier as a result.

Example 5c

It's worth noting that all the slash chords are implied by what the bass guitar and piano are doing. For a fully developed understanding of the harmony, you could try adding the missing bass note with your thumb. Without the C in the bass, the Bb/C will simply sound and feel like a Bb major chord, for example.

The next groove is a bit more explicit with larger chords, but even here Nile tends to gravitate towards small string fragments. Lightness of touch in the fretting hand is especially important, as the bass notes can dominate. If anything, your picking hand should gravitate more towards the top part of each chord.

Example 5d

Claydes Charles Smith

In our first example, the rhythm on beat 3 is a classic Smith device that's good practice for your general rhythm skills. Try "ghosting" the initial downstroke in mid-air on the rest before the chord to help catch this in time. The end of bar two sees another of his favourite moves from A9 to A9sus (although note the names A9/E and Em11 are related to the bass guitar holding down a low E).

Example 5e

The next groove allows bass, clavinet and horns to do all the heavy lifting with an effective scratchy line that's almost a precursor to John Frusciante's style in Red Hot Chili Peppers. It's all about heavy muting on all strings apart from the 7th fret E, so use every spare finger to cover the unwanted open strings. It can be a temptation to mute these strings using the picking hand, but this will be at the expense of any rhythmic fluidity.

Example 5f

As with the previous example, the harmony in the next groove happens in the background while the guitar largely stays on the same idea throughout. High octaves are a classic Disco-era device, and the simplicity of the shape allows for some more interesting rhythms. There's a cool phrase of three that gets recycled a few times here (check out the rhythm of the first three beats). Odd, non-linear phrasing like this can really transform simple ideas, because the ear is used to hearing groupings of 2, 4, 8 etc.

Example 5g

The octaves are based around the key of E for this example. If you'd like to play along with the piano part (and further your understanding of the harmony), here are the chords:

A E/G# F#m7

B B/F# B9sus

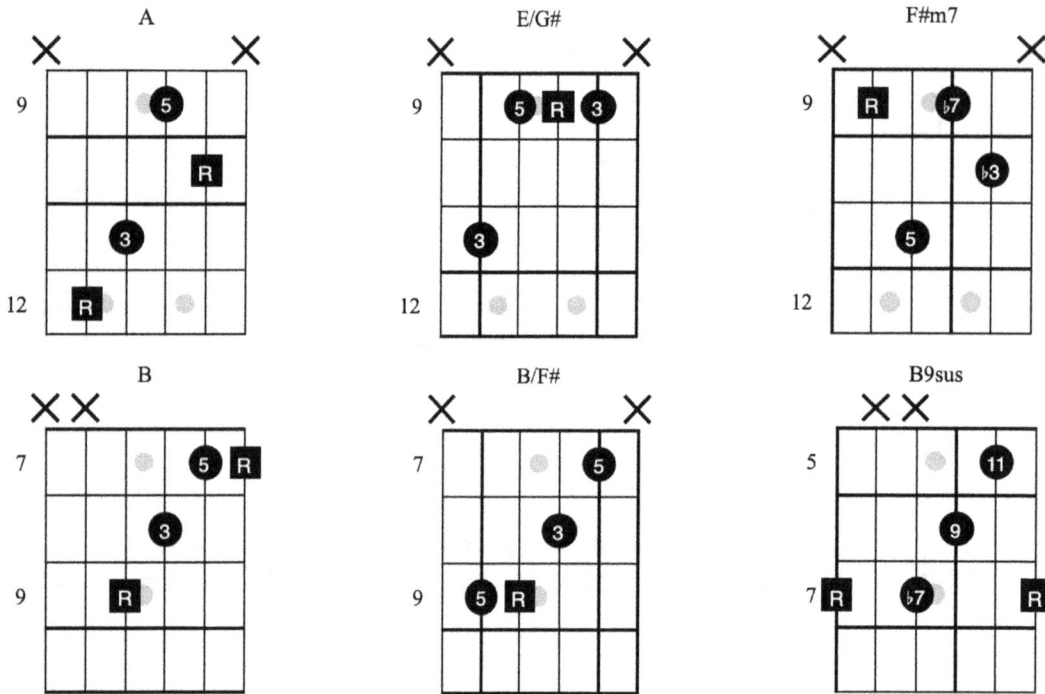

The final two grooves are based on the same chord sequence with the level of complexity ramping up in the second example. The chord progression follows a common idea that nails the b7 Mixolydian sound due to the bVII – I chord movement (bars one and two, and bars three and four). This progression is therefore D Mixolydian for two bars, then C Mixolydian for two, with the A7aug functioning as the V chord in D Major.

Example 5h

Cadd9/D   D

Bbadd9/C   C   A7aug

The next example tweaks the chords slightly, but it's the octave lines that are the challenge. We've already seen this Wes Montgomery scalic approach from Catfish Collins and it's a great way to expand your improvising skills in between chords. Since you can't look at both first and fourth fingers, aim to keep your focus on the fourth finger and trust that your fretting hand will maintain the octave shape as you move around the fretboard.

Example 5i

Al McKay

The next example can be played over the Example 5k backing track (and vice versa). It uses the typical *Foxy Lady* way of playing an Em7 close to the nut, so the treble really cuts through (especially when paired with a compressor pedal). There's a lot more syncopation and variation than meets the eye, so breaking down each bar with pick directions can really help.

Example 5j

The next groove is based upon a simple idea that McKay used to great effect on songs such as *Getaway*. The simple pivot from Em7 to the barred D/E (you can add the 5th string as well if you wish) is a great way to spice up static minor progressions.

Example 5k

The next two examples are typical intro and verse ideas (and are joined up for the backing). The first highlights Earth, Wind & Fire's Jazz-Fusion influence with slash chords and whole tone movement. Although McKay usually only plays the upper triad from these chords, it's worth exploring the "outside" sound of the full shape. The following E/D can be thought of as an alternative E dominant 7 chord, with the chord in third inversion (the b7 is the lowest note in the chord).

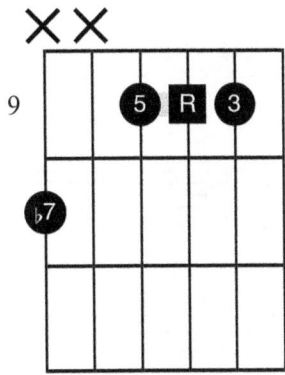

Example 51

The groove that follows uses double-stops mainly made up of 3rds. McKay uses a common Funk principle of improvising with 3rds constructed from chord tones (the D and Bm7, for example, both share the same chord tones of D and F#), plus another diatonic diad, either above or below this chord.

The main technical challenge is getting precise chords then mutes in all the correct places. Rather than look at this as a precise picking line, treat it like most of the Funk grooves we've studied, where the picking hand is loose and not resting on the strings/body of the guitar. This does make avoiding the lower open strings more of a challenge, so try adjusting the picking arc so that you're striking slightly into the body from the third string (rather than flatter, across all six strings).

Example 5m

This riff also uses a Bbmaj7 chord borrowed from the *parallel minor* key of D minor. This is a very common songwriting technique that involves temporarily jumping to a parallel key (or more accurately parallel mode), which allows us to play any of the chords from that mode. Most commonly this happens between major (Ionian) and minor (Aeolian), but we can do it between any mode. If you look at the chords of D Major and D Minor side by side, you should be able to see that alphabetically they are very similar. It's this proximity that allows us to make the jump from one side to the other:

D Major	D	Em	F#m	G	A	Bm	C#°
D Minor	Dm	E°	F	Gm	Am	Bb	C

The final example is a beautifully satisfying McKay-style chord progression combined with Soul and RnB ideas. It's largely diatonic to C Major/A Minor, although note that the E7(#9) harmonic twist doesn't need any special scalic treatment (simple diatonic 3rds sound great).

Example 5n

Chapter Six – Pop Funk

The players: David Williams, Paul Jackson Jnr., Prince.

Chapter Overview: Single note Funk lines, quartal harmony, diatonic 3rds.

The King of Pop, Michael Jackson needs no introduction as one of the most culturally important musicians of the 20th century. Even before he became a global solo phenomenon in the 1980s, he was a child star as lead singer of The Jackson Five. While the family band will be remembered for such hits as *ABC, I Want You Back* and *I'll Be There*, their post-Motown albums (now rebranded as The Jacksons) *Destiny* and *Triumph* captured more of the Disco/Funk craze of the late '70s. These albums produced such hits as *Shake Your Body (Down to the Ground), Lovely One, Blame It On The Boogie* and *Can You Feel It* that neatly bookend Michael's huge solo release *Off The Wall* from 1979. All these albums employed a huge roster of some of the finest producers, songwriters and session musicians on the circuit. Here I'm focusing on two of his funkiest session guitarists, David Williams and Paul Jackson Jnr., both of whom featured prominently from *Destiny* right up until Michael's eighth studio album, *Dangerous* (1991).

David Williams is arguably *the* most important single-note Funk guitarist in this book, yet he remains largely unknown, even in some guitar circles. His spanky, syncopated and often intricate lines have graced some of the biggest hits of all time, including *Billie Jean, Thriller, Bad* and *Smooth Criminal*. At a time of Hair-Metal and Neoclassical Shred, Williams eschewed the virtues of the "rhythm solo", exemplified in his short lead break in *Billie Jean*. This characteristic pentatonic-based style led him to become one of the most sought after behind-the-scenes session guitarists of the '80s and '90s, and he featured on a mind-bending number of hits from Madonna to Mariah Carey.

Williams used a variety of guitars, but his trusty Strat-style Ibanez Roadstar was his main one for many years. The classic out of phase "in between" position four on a Strat tends to be perfect for getting close to his unique sound. There are also plenty of Michael Jackson recordings with a healthy dose of compression on the guitar sound too. Williams apparently used the legendary Dumble ODS for several of MJ's recordings, but like Nile Rodgers, it's possible he also recorded direct through the desk with a healthy dose of compression.

Paul Jackson Jnr. was one of the most prolific L.A. session guitarists of the 1970s and '80s, performing alongside Michael Jackson, the Temptations, Luther Vandross, Bobby Womack, the Pointer Sisters, Chicago and Whitney Houston, among many others. His credits are truly astonishing, and even extend beyond the classic session player era of the '80s into the modern day with bands such as Daft Punk and The Weeknd. He featured as the in-house guitarist on *The Tonight Show With Jay Leno* and *American Idol* and also somehow managed to find time to launch his own solo career, with his unique brand of Smooth/Urban Jazz on albums such as *I Came To Play* and *Stories From Stompin' Willie*.

Like any consummate session pro, PJJR has used a huge variety of different guitars, including Valley Arts, Fender Telecasters, a Gibson ES-335 and Les Paul, Ibanez GB-10 and PRS guitars. His Valley Arts Strat-style guitar was the main guitar throughout his early session career, used in conjunction with Rivera amps. PJJR has always compressed his clean sound (starting with the MXR Dynacomp and later graduating to a rackmount dbx 160X in his Bob Bradshaw system).

Prince is another of the world's most iconic artists who shouldn't need any introduction. His output was truly prolific, releasing an astounding 39 albums during his lifetime. It's also believed that his infamous "vault" contains a vast amount of previously unreleased album material and music videos, so it's likely he'll be posthumously releasing material for years to come. However, it's his Funk credentials that I'm concentrating on here.

Prince helped to pioneer the *Minneapolis Sound* in the late '70s, a Funk-Rock subgenre that mixed in elements of New Wave and Synth Pop. Even through the artistic changes in his career, there's an identifiable Funk undercurrent on every single album. Whether it's a more traditional James Brown-style groove on songs such as *The Work Pt.1*, or post-70s Funk classics such as *Head* and *Controversy*, Prince's Funk guitar work shouldn't be overlooked in the context of his incredible songwriting.

Early on in Prince's career he used a modified Fender Telecaster and A Gibson L6S, before graduating to a Hohner Madcat in 1982 (a Tele copy) and, of course, the infamous Jerry Auerswald "Love Symbol" and David Rusan "Cloud" guitars. Amp-wise, Prince originally used Soldano SLO-100 and Orange AD140HTC heads.

Further Listening:

(David Williams)

Shake Your Body (Down To The Ground) – The Jacksons

Lovely One – The Jacksons

Rock With You – Michael Jackson

Thriller – Michael Jackson

Smooth Criminal – Michael Jackson

(Paul Jackson Jnr.)

P.Y.T – Michael Jackson

I Came To Play – Paul Jackson Jnr.

It's A Shame – Paul Jackson Jnr.

The Workout – Paul Jackson Jnr.

(Prince)

Soft and Wet – Prince

Lady Cab Driver – Prince

Kiss – Prince

David Williams

The first two examples use William's classic snappy single note style. This sound mainly comes from the sound of the strings hitting the frets, so you need plenty of force from the picking hand wrist to make this happen (this doesn't mean pulling the strings away from the guitar body, however).

Example 6a

The second idea builds upon the first with some rhythmic variation and extra notes from A Minor.

Example 6b

The next groove builds on the rhythmic concepts and syncopation seen in the first two examples, but this time using the B Mixolydian scale. Bars two and four see some deeper level syncopation and picking technique, however, with a couple of phrases that start on the offbeat 1/16th note upstroke. This riff also uses an Em7 chord borrowed from the parallel key of B Minor, the same technique that we looked at in the previous chapter. Here are the chords of B Mixolydian and B Aeolian so you can see where the Em7 chord comes from:

B Mixolydian	B	C#m	D#°	E	F#m	G#m	A
B Aeolian	Bm	C#°	D	Em	F#m	G	A

Whenever the jump from one mode to another happens, we need to use the appropriate scale for the new mode. In this case it means a slight tweak to the melody in bar four, with notes from the B Aeolian scale working over the Em7 section.

Example 6c

The final groove really plays upon the trickier offbeat 1/16th note rhythm from the previous example. This is where it really pays to have a strong sense of landing on the downbeat mute, as this will help you anticipate the offbeat notes.

Example 6d

Paul Jackson Jnr.

The main feature of this first groove is the Am11 shape that's played with the 3rd and 4th fingers (the 4th finger should be barred over the top two strings). This shape is derived from a concept known as *quartal harmony*. In traditional harmony, 3rds are stacked to create triads, 7th chords and so on. In quartal harmony, fourths are stacked on top of each other creating a slightly ambiguous suspended sound that's great for improvising in many styles including Funk. Here's the A Minor scale stacked in fourths using three note chords:

It's important to note that these shapes should all be viewed as "improvising options" within A Minor (or C Major) rather than assigning them specific chord names. The lack of a 3rd means that each chord can be named multiple ways, depending on what the background harmony is doing.

Example 6e

The next idea uses diatonic 3rds from C Dorian and tasteful Jazz-Blues lead lines to spice up the groove. Using different string groupings for 3rds is a very typical Paul Jackson idea that can help us to view the fretboard as one continuous note pool, rather than taking the typical "zonal" approach to scales.

Example 6f

The final PJJR groove is a masterclass in using diatonic 3rds (this time in G Major) all over the fretboard. He's a real master of improvising like this and it shows the power of learning these shapes in every key. Take note of the quick transition between the two shapes during beat 3 of bar one, as it can only be done at this speed with your first and second fingers.

Example 6g

Prince

Many of Prince's funk grooves are based around sparse two- and three-note chords that leave plenty of space for call and response between guitar and vocal/synth. The first rhythmic figure in bar one is an idea that crops up throughout his huge body of work. It can also be seen as a higher version of the typical bluesy Sly Stone style idea that we looked at in Chapter Four. The next two grooves are interchangeable over the same A Minor backing track, so you can mix and match or come up with your own ideas.

Example 6h

The minor 11 shape that we looked at with Paul Jackson Jnr. features heavily in the next riff. Most of the ideas are based around the closed A Minor Pentatonic shape in 5th position, but the extra major 6th (F#) provides that classic Prince twist, especially at the end of bar four.

Example 6i

Example 6j

The final groove is another great lesson in space, proving that you don't need a constant stream of 1/16th notes to sound funky. There's also some interesting harmonic ambiguity with the Am6 and D7sus4 chords looking like D7 and Am11 under the fingers. As always, many chords can be viewed from several different angles depending on what the underlying harmony/bass is doing.

Chapter Seven – Funk Rock

The players: P-Funk, John Frusciante, Nuno Bettencourt.

Chapter overview: Diminished 7 substitution, rhythmic displacement, Drop-D Funk.

Although the fusion of Funk and Rock might seem like an obvious next step in Funk's evolution, it only started to blossom at the beginning of the 1970s and can largely be traced back to the ashes of *The Jimi Hendrix Experience*. Hendrix's harder, more guitar-driven (and often more distorted) sound drew upon the zeitgeist of the late '60s and his new project *Band of Gypsies* started to blend elements of Funk, Soul and Rock. The band was a huge influence on the music of Curtis Mayfield, the Isley Brothers and Parliament-Funkadelic, and literally became the foundation of Hip-Hop. Funk Rock's development also partly reflected breakthroughs in technology (the first commercially available fuzz pedal didn't appear until 1962, for instance). Amps were also becoming bigger and louder, and this was mirrored in the music.

This mishmash of Psychedelia, Rock, RnB, Soul and Funk is probably best represented by George Clinton's Parliament-Funkadelic collective. Originally starting out as a doo-wop band, then morphing into a rocky RnB outfit, it was Funkadelic's seminal album *Maggot Brain* (1971) that put the band on its psychedelic Funk Rock trajectory. Guitarist Eddie Hazel's fret-melting fuzz-soaked guitar solos were introduced to the world alongside the funky chank of Tawl Ross. Together, they provided much of the guitar-based blueprint for Clinton's projects. The sister bands Parliament and Funkadelic can be loosely divided into radio-friendly commercial Funk versus more Psychedelic Rock and, over time, *P-Funk* has come to represent the entire collective of musicians and bands within Clinton's sphere, as well as the mythology that surrounds it. It's hard to understate the extraordinary influence this revolving door of over 50 incredible musicians has had on both Rock and Funk. The guitar roster over the years has included the likes of Hazel, Garry "Diaper Man" Shider, Ron Brykowski, and Michael "Kid Funkadelic" Hampton among many others.

The style focus here is on the rhythm playing of these core guitarists during Funkadelic's most successful period in the 1970s, so roughly covers the albums from *Maggot Brain* (1971) to *One Nation Under a Groove* (1978). It can be notoriously difficult to tell who played what due to the frequent guest appearances and lack of album credits, so I've gone for some of the grittier/rockier and swirly psychedelic tones that characterised the P-Funk sound. Since Hazel set the stage for all future guitarists, his holy trinity of Strat, fuzz and phaser is a great place to start.

After a brief hiatus in the '80s, Funk Rock had a revival during the '90s with the likes of Jane's Addiction, Faith No More, Primus, Living Colour and Rage Against the Machine, all blending Funk with more aggressive Rock and Metal styles. Perhaps the best-known and most successful band in this field was the Red Hot Chili Peppers. The band's long association with Funk started with the George Clinton-produced *Freaky Styley* (1985), but it wasn't until *Mother's Milk* (1989) and *Blood Sugar Sex Magik* (1991) that the four-piece line-up of Anthony Keidis (vocals), Flea (bass), Chad Smith (drums) and John Frusciante (guitar) was solidified, and their confident blend of Punk Rock and Funk launched them into superstardom. The albums that followed (including when Dave Navarro stepped into Frusciante's shoes for *One Hot Minute*) all feature Funk to some extent, but it's the funky zenith of *Blood Sugar Sex Magik* that I'll be mainly focusing on here.

Unlike most of the guitarists in this book, Frusciante wasn't well-schooled in the ways of Funk before joining the band. Although he was a fan of P-Funk's Eddie Hazel, his main influences revolved around Page, Beck, Hendrix and Zappa, so he learned most of his groove and Funk style from emulating the playing the Chili's late guitarist Hilell Slovak who died from a drugs overdose in 1988.

Frusciante originally played a lot of vintage Fenders on the first Chili Peppers albums, including a 1966 Jaguar and a 1958 Stratocaster. Amp-wise, he started out with Carvin and Soldano heads, but later graduated to vintage Marshall tones with amps such as the Marshall JCM800 and Jubilee. For distorted tones, the Boss DS-2 was used and the MXR Dynacomp was added for some of those squishy clean sounds (think of the clean solo on *Mellowship Slinky in B Major*).

The band Extreme breathed some fresh life into a waning Soft Rock/Hair Metal genre during the '90s, largely through the prodigious songwriting and technical prowess of guitarist Nuno Bettencourt. Although well-versed in the gymnastic rock playing of guitarists such as Eddie Van Halen, Bettencourt brought a funky edge to this style, particularly on the early albums *Extreme II: Pornograffitti* (1990), *III Sides to Every Story* (1992) and *Waiting for the Punchline* (1995).

During the early Extreme period, Bettencourt played his signature Washburn N4 guitars through the very popular ADA MP-1 preamp into a Macintosh transistor poweramp with some extra EQ excitement courtesy of a rackmount BBE Sonic Maximiser. This was producer Michael Wagener's go-to sound for SkidRow's first album and White Lion's *Pride*. Nuno also used Eb tuning for an even fatter rock sound (but here the examples are recorded at concert pitch to avoid the need to retune your guitar). A bridge humbucker into some high output valve distortion with a fairly flat midrange EQ will get you close to the right sound.

Further Listening:

Red Hot Mama – Funkadelic

Standing On The Verge of Getting It On – Funkadelic

Good to Your Earhole – Funkadelic

Loose Booty – Funkadelic

Cholly (Funk Getting Ready to Roll!) – Funkadelic

Give Up The Funk – Parliament

Flashlight – Parliament

Higher Ground – Red Hot Chili Peppers

Give It Away – Red Hot Chili Peppers

If You Have To Ask – Red Hot Chili Peppers

Suck My Kiss – Red Hot Chili Peppers

Mellowship Slinky in B Major – Red Hot Chili Peppers

Can't Stop – Red Hot Chili Peppers

Get The Funk Out – Extreme

Cynical – Extreme

Cupid's Dead – Extreme

Slide – Extreme

P-Funk

This first groove spends a lot of time on the offbeat 1/16th note, and there are a lot of upstrokes and syncopation as a result. Note the rests in between each of these offbeats; ensure the notes are cut off in staccato fashion using the fretting hand. Once again, we're using F# Mixolydian to highlight the sound of the F#9 chord.

Example 7a

The next groove combines a nice octave pattern with an ascending C Dorian/C Minor Pentatonic idea. The octave line on beat two starts with a downstroke/upstroke and therefore requires a challenging *inside picking* technique, whereby you pick on the "inside" of the two strings.

Example 7b

The next groove is a great exercise in strumming precision and coordination between the two hands. Although it's a simple I – V chord movement, the challenge is really nailing the rest and the precise grouping of chords. Like much of the 1/16th note-based Funk in this book, this is a case of selectively playing on downstrokes or upstrokes. You will benefit from practicing smaller portions of the bar (e.g. repeat the first A9 phrase up to beat "2&") to help focus on the interaction between the two hands.

As always, no matter what, keep the picking hand moving at all times in a steady 1/16th note motion.

Example 7c

The next groove is all about economy of movement and space. Aim for precision with the rests, as these are just as important as the chords and try not to keep time with any kind of muting or "chopping" onto the strings with the picking hand.

Example 7d

The final P-Funk groove draws upon several of the concepts we've looked at, including 1/16th pushed rhythms and syncopation, but this riff really milks the offbeat 1/16th note rhythm. This is designed to be the type of "scat" style unison vocal/guitar melody (think of George Benson) that was very common in Funkadelic tracks.

As such, it can be great to learn the melody with your voice before going anywhere near the guitar, as this can really help to bed in the offbeat rhythms and understand how they anticipate the strong beats.

Example 7e

John Frusciante

The first Chili Peppers-style groove combines the Cheese Martin minor 6 idea from Chapter One with Frusciante's typical single note approach. His style is often based around lots of picking hand movement through all the strings but isolating only the single notes. This means flattening any spare fretting hand fingers and using the thumb to mute the unwanted lower open E and A strings.

Example 7f

The next groove highlights how Frusciante often visualises his chordal improvising around minor pentatonic shapes. Take note of the 10th, 12th and 13th fret chord cluster in bar two, for example. You can visualise this as part of the D Dorian scale with the added b5 from the Blues scale. At its heart, it's simply part of the classic "shape one" D Blues scale.

Example 7g

The next groove shows Frusciante's rockier side with some Hendrix style Em, Bm and Cm chord ideas. I think he probably views these as *Foxy Lady* style dominant 7(#9) chords, even though there's no explicit major 3rd inside the shape. Bar two also has a nice idea that can be seen as rockier development of Steve Cropper 6ths. This sliding approach is very effective when using distortion as there's no bleed between the notes (major 3rds and 6ths can sound slightly out of tune when using distortion).

Example 7h

The final groove uses a simple i – V7 (Em – B7) chord progression but uses a D# diminished 7 chord which is a great substitute for B7. This jazzy diminished 7 substitution is built upon the 3rd degree of the V7 chord. As you can see here, D# diminished 7 shares three notes with B7 and this one of the main reasons it works:

Interval:	1	3	5	b7	b9
B7:	B	D#	F#	A	
D#°7:		D#	F#	A	C

The D# also helps the chord resolve really well to the following chord. When these two chords are combined (i.e., B D# F# A C), it spells out a B7(b9) chord, a subtle variation on the dominant 7(#9) we've looked at many times throughout this book.

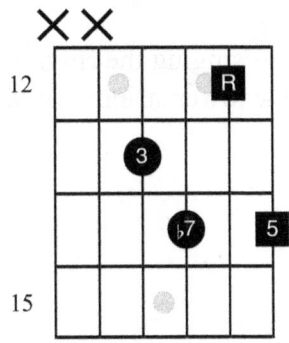

B7

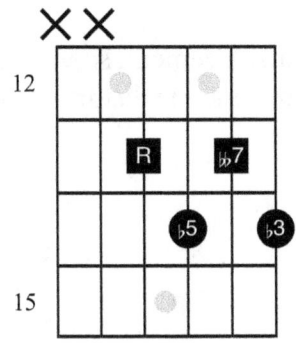

D#°7

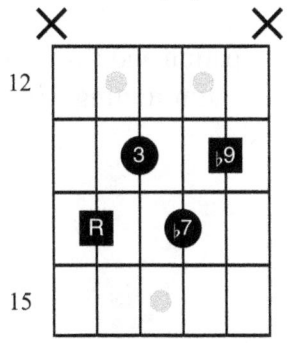

B7(b9)

Example 7i

Nuno Bettencourt

This first riff combines some tricky syncopation and rhythmic displacement, so vocalising/singing the rhythm can work well before trying this on guitar. Palm-muting will help tame the distortion on the lower strings while giving a punchier, more percussive sound.

Example 7j

The next riff is based around the E Minor Pentatonic scale and should be short and punchy to mimic the sound of horns. Much of the syncopation falls on the offbeat 1/16th note rhythm, so this should see you land on upstrokes if you're following strict alternate picking.

Example 7k

Nuno was a big fan of Drop-D tuning combined with the fatter, warmer sound of the neck pickup. This tuning leads to a convenient first and third fingering that will allow you to easily play the D Minor Pentatonic scale in third position.

Example 71

Chapter Eight – Modern Funk

The players: Adam Smirnoff/Eric Krasno, Mark Lettieri, Cory Wong.

Chapter overview: Combining parallel scales, fingerstyle Funk, cycle progressions, baritone Funk, applying bass technique to guitar.

With a back catalogue of nearly seventy years of great Funk music, it's no surprise that modern guitar players often reference the guitarists featured in this book. Funk has seen something of a revival recently with newer, younger audiences being turned onto classic Funk through the skilful blend of old-school Funk with other genres such as Hip-Hop, Gospel and Jazz.

Lettuce have been at the forefront of championing modern, largely instrumental Funk ever since their debut *Outta Here* in 2002. Formed by a group of likeminded Berklee undergrads in the '90s, the band has managed to function as a part-time project to this day, with all its members earning their session stripes with the likes of Lady Gaga, Kanye West and Justin Timberlake. Guitarists Adam Smirnoff and Eric Krasno provide the backbone to the Boston Funk collective, fusing Hip-Hop, Soul, Jazz, Dub and Rock to keep their sound fresh and cutting edge.

Smirnoff has been the only regular guitarist in the band since 2015 and like one of his major influences, Bruce Conte, he plays a VOS 1960 Les Paul rather than the typical Fender Strat/Tele. His amp of choice is a Fender Twin, together with a selection of effects pedals including a Mu-tron Octavider, MXR Phase 90, Ibanez Tubescreamer and Crybaby Wah.

Krasno's career includes writing and playing with the Tedeschi Trucks Band, producing 50 Cent, and also co-founding the Soul-Fusion outfit Soulive. Suffice to say that his playing and sound is eclectic! Early on he played a Strat, later switching to a Gibson ES-335 that he played on the majority of Lettuce and Soulive gigs. In the mid '00s he helped to produce his signature Ibanez EKM100 with a Bigsby trem. For Lettuce recordings, Krasno kept things simple, normally just playing into a Mesa/Boogie Lonestar 2x12 combo with gain and boost pedals for different gain stages.

Mark Lettieri started out in the RnB and Gospel scene of the Dallas/Fort Worth area of Texas, and this eventually led to him joining the instrumental Jazz/World group Snarky Puppy. In 2018, Lettieri joined up with The Fearless Flyers, featuring Cory Wong and Joe Dart of Vulfpeck on guitar and bass, and drummer Nate Smith. He also has six solo releases to date and a thriving online community through YouTube where he regularly showcases new material. As an in-demand session guitarist he has recorded and toured with the likes of Erikah Badu, Nelly, Anthony Evans, 50 Cent, David Crosby and Kirk Franklin. Inevitably, his style is eclectic, blending Rock, Jazz, Gospel and Funk. Early Rock influences, such as Hendrix, EVH and Joe Satriani, later gave way to Jazz with artists such as John Scofield and Herbie Hancock, all the way to Funk with Prince, Stevie Wonder and James Brown.

Lettieri started out on Strats and Teles, eventually graduating to his own signature PRS Fiore. He also uses a multitude of baritone guitars including Danelectro and PRS. Sitting somewhere between a bass and a guitar (normally tuned low to high B E A D F# B), this tuning seems to lend itself very well to groove-based Funk. You could technically detune a conventional guitar, but you'd have use a heavy gauge string set such as 12-60 to avoid tuning issues and flapping strings. He uses several amps including Fender Princeton, Fender Hot Rod Deville, Naylor Duel 60 and Supro Statesman heads, and also a Kemper Profiling Head for recording.

Cory Wong is a guitarist from the Vulfpeck and Fearless Flyers stable, who has released several solo albums and collaborated with Dirty Loops. Early influences include David Williams and Paul Jackson Jnr. as well as usual suspects such as Nile Rodgers, which is reflected in his particularly rubbery and loose picking hand wrist.

Cory isn't particularly fussy about specific gear, so you'll see him using amps such as the Roland JC-120 Jazz Chorus, a Fender Twin, through to the Kemper digital profiler (emulating '65 Fender Super Reverb and '64 Fender Vibroverb amps), and even stock Logic Pro X amp plugins. Although he now uses his signature Cory Wong Strat, for years he used the relatively cheap Highway One Strat fitted with Seymour Duncan Antiquity Surf pickups for punchy cleans. He is very much a Strat "position 4" guy, however, and this is key to his glassy, upfront sound (to the point where he has a "4th position panic switch" fitted to his signature Strat). Similarly, compression is crucial in emulating Cory's sound, though he favours using compressors with a blend knob (such as the Wampler Ego) rather than a fully compressed sound. This allows some of the natural dynamics to come through, with the squashed compressor sound sitting underneath.

Further Listening:

Squadlive – Lettuce

Nyack (Live) – Lettuce

Relax – Lettuce

Get Greasy – Lettuce

One in Seven – Soulive

Gigantactis – Mark Lettieri

Barreleye – Mark Lettieri

Pulsar – Mark Lettieri

Jefe – Snarky Puppy

Assassin – Cory Wong

Lilypad – Cory wong

Swampers – The Fearless Flyers

3 On E – Vulfpeck

Adam Smirnoff/Eric Krasno

The first groove is a typical Smirnoff style I – IV vamp that heavily references Bruce Conte's style. The main technique focus here is the quick 1/32nd rhythm in bars one and three. Aim to crescendo through these chords into the beat 4, going from a small to wide picking movement.

Example 8a

Krasno's style tends to be more on the Jimmy Nolen side of the street, with funky single note lines that sound great close to the bridge. This idea also "plays the changes" (i.e., switches between Eb and Ab Mixolydian accordingly).

Example 8b

The next riff is a greasy Krasno-style groove that combines the vibe of Leo Nocentelli with the jazzier vocabulary of John Scofield. It weaves in between parallel Bb scales (Major/Minor Pentatonic, Blues and Mixolydian), with the chromatic passing notes coming from jumping between these scales. To bring this out in your own playing, you'll need to start by practising these scales individually in one position. As you become more comfortable with the shapes, try sliding between notes that aren't common (e.g., the 4th fret Db at the end of bar one is taken from Bb Minor Pentatonic, but isn't present within Bb Major Pentatonic or Bb Mixolydian).

Example 8c

Smirnoff often effortlessly blends Gospel, Soul and Dub ideas within his Funk playing and this final Lettuce-style groove features all these styles in quick succession. The palm-muted triplet in bar four is a typical Reggae/Dub-style rhythm, for example, and sounds great against the straight 1/8th rhythm in the background. This should have the feeling of "putting on the brakes" and is an excellent way to create rhythmic interest.

Example 8d

Mark Lettieri

This first groove is based around Lettieri's baritone Funk concept and is approached almost as if it was a bassline. The "shake" at the end of bar two is a technique lifted directly from electric bass technique. Rather than trilling the normal two-fingered legato way, this technique involves sliding the fretting hand rapidly from side to side. The first finger works best, with the thumb disengaged from the back of the neck to allow for a floating hand position. Bar four also features his signature "pitchwheel" effect that requires similarly fast sideways fretting hand movement.

If you don't have a way to play this using low B baritone tuning, I've provided a backing track in standard tuning.

Example 8e

The final Lettieri-style riff shows off some of his dextrous fingerstyle technique and Gospel chord chops. As with the previous groove, this borrows some technique ideas from bass guitar and introduces the more guitar-orientated *rest slap* denoted by "RS" (the picking hand naturally comes to rest on the strings rather than executing an overt bass style slap). All of the ghost notes "(X)" and rest slap indications use this technique to varying degrees of strength and adding the thumb will accentuate the percussive sound.

Example 8f

Cory Wong

This first groove effortlessly blends Gospel harmony with a Funk backbone. "Wongisms" include chromatic 3rds and palm-muted, thumbed double-stops. It's fingerstyle, and not only allows for some wider interval chords, but the thumb can be used as a further rhythmic device (all the thumb mutes on the low E string use the rest slap idea used in the previous Mark Lettieri example).

Example 8h

The next groove brings back the pat technique introduced in Example 4m and intersperses some traditional Funk chord fragments with improvised diads. The lick in bar four can be largely viewed through the lens of a basic E Major Pentatonic scale shape (although slightly tweaked to catch the D natural from E Mixolydian).

Example 8i

```
        Pat  E7        Eb7    E7        Eb9  E9          Pat  E7        Eb7   E7
                                           8———9·X—X—
                                           8———9·X—X—
T———————X—5—X—X———4—X———5———X—X—8———9·X—X—————X—5—X—X———4—X—5—X—————————————————
A———————X—7—X—X———6—X———7———X—X—8———9·X—X—————X—7—X—X———6—X—7—X—2—X—3—4—X—X———————
B———————X—6—X—X———5—X———6———X—X—————————————————X—6—X—X———5—X—6—X—4—X—5—6—X—X———————
    ————0—X—————————————————————————————0—X———————————————————————————————————————
```

```
        Pat  E7        Eb7   E7                Pat  E7        Eb7    N.C.
                                                                      P.M. - - - - - - - - - - -
                                                               12—
T———————X—5—X—X———4—X———5—X—11—12—X—————————————X—5—X—X———4—X—8———9—12—9——————————
A———————X—7—X—X———6—X———7—X—12—13—X—————————————X—7—X—X———6—X—8———9—11—9——11—9—————
B———————X—6—X—X———5—X———6—X——————————X—X————————X—6—X—X———5—X—————————————12—9—9———
    ————0—X—————————————————————————X—X—————0—X————————————————————————————11—————
```

The final example travels through four different keys in a familiar harmonic movement that descends in 5ths. This kind of chord progression is known as a *cycle progression* as it closely moves through part of the Cycle of Fifths used to identify sharp/flat keys.

This groove shows four unique approaches to playing over a dominant 7 chord, so they can easily be interchanged or even transposed to other keys. I'd suggest practicing each bar as an entirely separate phrase then transposing each into a new position/key (e.g., the A7 idea could be moved up two fret positions and work over B7).

Example 8j

Unusually, Cory has a closed picking hand (fingers tucked together) for single note and double-stop picking and more open/splayed for the 1/16th note strumming. This seems to allow for more precision on palm-mutes and smaller shapes, while the splayed fingers are possibly acting as a counterbalance. This might also be a side effect of really relaxing the picking hand wrist to the point where the only tension is between the thumb and index finger in order to grip the pick.

Chapter Nine – Resources

Tone Vault

I had the luxury of using several different guitars when recording the audio for this book, each of which lends its own sound, character and playing style to cover the main guitar groups.

- *Strat players:* Fender Relic Custom Shop 62 with rosewood fingerboard, oval C-shape neck and '60s style pickups

- *Hollow body players:* Gibson ES-335 '63 VOS fitted with Bareknuckle Mule pickups

- *Les Paul players:* Gibson Custom 1958 Les Paul Standard Reissue VOS with C-shape mahogany neck and Custombucker Alnico III pickups

- *Telecaster players:* American Deluxe Telecaster fitted with Bareknuckle Yardbird pickups

- I also played a selection of other guitars including a Gibson Firebird 2014 Classic, Musicman Axis Super Sport and a Danelectro '59 Reissue Baritone

- All the amp sounds were recorded via either a Fender Deluxe Reverb or Victory V40 Duchess, through a Two Notes Torpedo Live loadbox (with a selection of Twin, Super Reverb and Victory IRs) and recorded into Logic via an Audient iD14 interface. I used very minimal EQ, but I often used Waves API-2500 and dbx 160 compressor plugins

Like most guitarists I have far too many pedals, but for this book I used the following:

- Analogman King of Tone and JHS AT+ drive pedals

- MXR Script Phase 90

- Analogman Chorus

- Beetronics Octahive, Chasetone '69 Red Velvet and Tate FX fuzz pedals

- Wampler Ego compressor

Further listening

I genuinely hope you derive as much pleasure playing through these grooves and discovering the world of Funk as I had writing and recording this book. As I said at the beginning of this Funk odyssey, active listening will not only help you understand the rhythmic and harmonic language of Funk but allow you to develop as a musician and find your own voice.

I'd also encourage you to develop the discipline of transcribing by ear, as this will help promote even deeper listening skills. I learned a huge amount just by digging into the intricacies of players such as Nile Rodgers. Before I knew it, I'd absorbed so much technique, approaches to rhythm, and vocabulary that it allowed me to apply these in many other situations.

The beautiful thing about music is that there's always more to discover and learn. The following playlist contains over 20 hours of great Funk music and includes some of the players/bands that I would have loved to have included in the book but simply didn't have room for. By all means use it as a Funk music encyclopedia, but I hope you'll also use it as a platform for your own discoveries.

Finally, there are some lessons, tips and general guitar geekery on my website **steveallsworth.com** as well as videos and more in-depth explanations of some of the concepts from this book. I'd love to see you over there!

Connect with Steve:

Instagram: **@steveallsworthguitar**

YouTube: **Steve Allsworth**

www.ingramcontent.com/pod-product-compliance
Lightning Source LLC
Chambersburg PA
CBHW081431090426
42740CB00017B/3270